With
a
Closed
fist

To Elizabeth,

Thank you for
coming!
Kathy Bohm

With a Closed Fist

Growing up in Canada's Toughest
Neighbourhood

KATHY DOBSON

Véhicule Press

Published with the generous assistance of The Canada Council for the Arts and the Canada Book Fund of the Department of Canadian Heritage.

Cover and title design: David Drummond
Cover photograph: Gabor Szilasi
Painting on last page: Scott Dobson-Mitchell

Set in Adobe Minion and MrsEaves by Simon Garamond

Printed by Marquis Book Printing Inc.

LIBRARY AND ARCHIVES CANADA CATALOGUING IN PUBLICATION
Dobson, Kathy
With a closed fist : growing up in Canada's toughest neighbourhood / Kathy Dobson.

Includes bibliographical references and index.
ISBN 978-1-55065-323-6

1. Dobson, Kathy—Childhood and youth.
2. Pointe-Saint-Charles (Montréal, Québec)—Biography.
3. Poor families—Québec (Province)—Montréal—Biography.
I. Title.

FC2947.26.D63A3 2011   971.4'28092   C2011-905455-8

Published by Véhicule Press, Montréal, Québec, Canada
www.vehiculepress.com

Distribution in Canada by LitDistCo
orders@litdistco.ca

Distribution in U.S. by Independent Publishers Group
www.ipgbook.com

Printed in Canada on FSC certified paper.

To my sisters,

who always had my back

Acknowledgements

It was on Mother's Day, 2006, when my mother drew her last breath. A couple of my sisters still say she did it on purpose. It would be so like our mother to choose that day to die, knowing she was on her way out anyway, after a lengthy battle with Lewy Body Dementia.

"Say what you need to say and then put a period at the end of it," my mother would often say. Mother's Day 2006 became her period, I guess. While writing her eulogy, I struggled to find just the right words to explain how hard she fought to give a voice to those who needed it most. I remembered how she stood in front of the Montréal Riot Squad, staring them down, while I shivered in fear at a safe distance, convinced she was about to get her teeth knocked out. When I told her later how much I had admired her fearlessness that day, she laughed. "I was scared shitless," she said. "But sometimes you have to do stuff, no matter how scary it seems."

I still sometimes feel like I'm lying when I tell people I actually found a real publisher who agreed to publish my book. When Simon Dardick said to me, during our first conversation about the book, "Now you need to go off and think about how you want to write it," he changed everything. Suddenly I was free to approach the book from whatever corner I thought best. Instead of using my journalist voice, I could just tell my stories straight up, in my own voice, as a kid growing up in the Point. Simon's faith in my voice made all the difference.

My agent Robert Lecker's insights and suggestions about how to best tell my story shaped the book's direction in many ways. I'll always count that phone call from him after he read the first draft as one of the favorite moments of my life. Thank you, Robert.

To my friend Christine, thanks for helping me get the French right. And to Linda Savory-Gordon, one of the people I love the most. My mom was right. You are the real deal.

And a special thanks to Jenny and Scott, my first readers, who laughed and cried in all the right places. And always told me the truth.

Speak up for those who cannot speak for themselves,
for the rights of all who are destitute.
Speak up and judge fairly;
defend the rights of the poor and needy.

–Proverbs 31: 8&9

Chapter One

I'VE ALWAYS LIVED IN FEAR of going to the bathroom. I know if I sit on the toilet for more than a couple of minutes, I risk having a rat crawl up the pipes and bite me on the ass. I stomp my feet, peeing as quickly as possible while singing "The Unicorn Song" so loudly my mom yells at me to stop yelling.

"A long time ago...when the Earth was green," I sing, then stomp.

"There was more kinds of animals than you've ever seen..." STOMP.

"They'd run around free while the Earth was being born..." STOMP. STOMP. "And the loveliest of all was the unicorn..."

My favourite part is about the Earth deciding to be born and the green alligators and long-necked geese.

"Some cats and rats and elephants, but sure as you're born... The loveliest of all was the unicorn."

Even the Irish Rovers agree that rats are low on the totem pole. Do the rats know I'm putting them down? Are they jealous of those unicorns?

Sometimes at night while lying in bed I can hear a rat trying to escape from the toilet, banging the inside of the lid with its head, trying to pop it open so it can climb out. I hate that banging noise. It means the sewers are backed up again and within a few hours we'll see more of the furry fuckers running around the apartment. Forget any peace negotiations or truces. I'd gladly push a button that kills every single rat on the planet in one shot, including the non-ass biting ones. If I only knew where that button was.

My mom says the rats are more afraid of me than I am of them. My mom is wrong. The rats—or at least Point St. Charles rats—are definitely not afraid of me. Or anyone. Hell, my mom has her own rat horror stories, including the time one stared her down after she accidentally got between it and its exit in the basement. She had walked downstairs to say goodnight to me and my sisters. That was when we lived in the one bedroom on Charlevoix Street and had all three of the bunk beds set up in the basement. After her foot hit the bottom step, Mom spotted the rat sniffing around under the basement's far window, the one closest to Ruth and Annie's bunk.

When she suddenly screamed, "YOU FUCKING BASTARD!" we all threw our blankets over our heads, knowing a rat must be somewhere in the basement with us.

"YOU FUCKING FURRY PRICK!" she shrieked, then grabbed the blanket off the edge of my bed. Great. With my face now exposed to the free roaming rat, I just knew it was going to jump and take a hunk out of my face. Instead, it jumped at my mom, who froze as it dashed right up the front of her body and jumped off her left shoulder. I swear to god it was squeaking the whole time. More scared of us my ass. I knew it was telling my mom to "BITE ME" in rat. My sisters finally pulled the blankets off their faces just in time to watch as our mom sank down onto the edge of my bunk bed. She had to sit for a good ten minutes before her legs would work again. Her voice still worked fine though as she ranted about all the filth and disease a rat brings and how the asswipes down at city hall needed to get their goddamn act together. "Nobody gives a shit about us in the Point," she'd say, explaining it was on account of our neighbourhood being filled with welfare bums and slum landlords. I knew she'd be on the phone the next morning, threatening to call the papers if the city didn't DO SOMETHING.

"I know you bastards are dumping shit into the sewers. My kids are all going to get asthma for Christ's sake. Even the rats don't like it and are coughing their fucking heads off. They're pouring out of the toilet and coming into our apartment again and I swear to God, if one of my kids get bitten…What? *Mange de la merd*e! Fuck you!"

She couldn't stop shuddering. I debated whether I had the nerve to ask her to read us a story. She had sent us to bed earlier without a story, hoping, I guess, that we wouldn't notice we didn't have anything for supper.

I have to admit, the mice in the Point aren't as bad as the rats. Sure, they'll shit and piss all over the place and chew a lot of wires and stuff, but unlike the rats they never bite any asses. Every once in a while a mouse will pop out of the toaster, or pour out of a Corn Flakes box and land with a clunk into the bowl, but at least they always run away quickly. I think they really are more afraid of us than we are of them. If anyone's ever been bitten by one, they aren't telling. One time my dad spotted something moving around under the small carpet near the front door and before my brain could even wonder what the hell it was, he ran over and punched it. While he rubbed his knuckles and called for the sons of bitches, my mom yelled at him for wrecking the carpet.

"Now it's garbage! Are you happy? It's GARBAGE!"

After we formed a tight huddle around the lump, my sister Ruth slowly peeled the carpet back. That mouse was so flattened, its guts were leaking through the top of the carpet. The tiny squished face with its bulging eyes and small pink tongue hanging out the side looked like a picture ripped from a colouring book. But with the colours already there. It stayed in my mind for a long time.

In the Point, you move for one of two reasons: the place is on fire or the rent is due. It seems like we're always putting out small fires. It's the smell that usually warns us first; a coppery burning smell that starts in the walls. One time, when small flames came licking out of the walls in the bathroom upstairs, like someone on the other side was shoving a knife of tiny flames through the paint, my mom first tried putting it out herself. But even I knew that her frantic cups of water and splashes from the bathtub weren't going to do it. We were all crying and begging her to call the fire department, but my mom hates calling them. She has to clean up before they can arrive. She told my Aunt Alice one time that she hates to see the looks between the fire fighters when they see how we're living, muttering about "firebugs" under their breath. I always try to see those looks whenever the firemen show up, wanting to know what my mom means. How are we living? Where do those firebugs in the walls come from? But they're too busy yelling at us in French to get the hell out for me to study their faces. Then Mom will stand on the sidewalk, trying to explain to all the gawking neighbours that it's on account of the bad wiring and those cheap slumlord bastards hiding out in their Westmount mansions, never fixing anything until one of their goddamn dumps goes up in flames.

"The bastards just want to collect their insurance money."

Sometimes the fires aren't because of bad wiring though. Sheds in the laneways usually catch on fire from matches. Me and my sister Julia watched some French kids setting Mr. Belvidere's shed on fire one day just after school. It went up so fast I couldn't believe it. The kids from the Catholic school threw some matches on an old mattress in the lane and just a few minutes later the flames were climbing the side of the building. The kids grinned at us and then took off.

Me and Julia just had time to run back down the other way before Mr. Belvidere came rushing out of his apartment, swinging his fists and yelling, "*C'est un FEU!* You little cocksuckers!"

We watched from across the street as some neighbours helped Mr. Belvidere drag some of his junk out until the fire department arrived. A stained mattress, a large TV, some kitchen chairs, and black garbage bags stuffed with clothing and blankets made a growing pile on the sidewalk in front of his building. In the back laneway, firemen whacked the shit out of the burning shed, hacking away at it with axes like it was a wild dog trying to eat them. Me and Julia kept running back and forth from the lane to the front, wondering if the fire was going to spread.

By now it seemed like half the kids from the Point were there. One of the firemen gave us dirty looks from across the street as he pulled more equipment off the truck. Like the asshole thought we were going to try and steal anything not nailed down. There wasn't anything worth ripping off from their stupid truck anyway. They were already wearing the good stuff. I wanted to tell the one with the hard stare that it wasn't us who had started the fire, it was a couple of stupid Pepsis from the Catholic school. He kept glaring and someone behind me yelled at him to get a real job, making us all laugh. He gave us the finger then turned away. Fuckers. They just hate us because of the Victoria Day bonfires. That's when the Point almost burns to the ground.

We lived in the one bedroom on Charlevoix Street for about three months until the landlord was ringing the doorbell all the time, banging on the front door and yelling for his rent. Our mom would shush us and we'd become so still we could hear the landlord talking to himself outside the front door.

"A family of garbage living in my house, that's what they are. Just pure garbage!"

That pissed Mom off so bad she yanked the front door open and demanded to know who Mr. Prick Head was calling garbage? After telling him where he could shove his eviction notice and explaining what a useless piece of shit he was since his apartment had rats, cockroaches and no running hot water, she slammed the door shut.

"There's lots of hot water!" Mr. Prick Head yelled through the door.

A few hours later, Mom was packing us up, ready to pull another midnight move.

"We can find a better place than this shit box, anyway," she always says.

The next day we moved to a three bedroom on Rozel Street. It's a lot bigger than our last place, but it's on the third floor and surrounded by French people. My sister Annie says it means the rats have two whole floors of Frenchie asses to bite through before they even reach any of ours. Annie is always finding the positive in everything. Of course, living in a nest of Frogs means a mini war every time we have to leave the apartment. Or try to get back in.

"Hey, you Peppers wanna move your fucking asses outta the way, *tabarnac*?"

It's something we have to go through almost every single day before and after school. At first they pretend not to hear us. Then they pretend not to understand "da hinglish" as we pretend not to understand the "frog-langue."

"*Maudit tête carré.*"

"Fuck you!"

"*Mange de la merde!*"

"Hey, the priest better suck you off a bit harder next time, eh?"

"*Ferme ta gueule!*"

And then the shoving match starts. Sometimes a mother opens a door somewhere and yells for us to stop. Depending on what language she's yelling in, half of us usually do.

Mom has started hanging around with hippies from McGill University. Every time she brings a new one home and introduces us, they always say the exact same thing.

"Your six girls are just like steps and ladders!"

Ruth had to explain it to us the first time, saying it was on account of each of us being born one year after another. If our baby brother Russell hadn't died right after he was born, our mom would have had a baby almost every single year. Ruth, Annie, me, Julia, Beth, and Hannah. Yup. That's us. Steps and ladders.

When I hear that some of the hippies are actually medical school students, I wonder if all doctors start out that way. You know, pretending to be poor and wanting to live in Point St. Charles even though they can live anywhere they want to in Montréal, including Westmount with the rest of the rich people. They've rented two upper floors on Wellington Street, knocking a hole in the wall between the two apartments, making it one large place they can go back and forth between. The freaks. Dad calls it their terrorist cell. But I don't think it looks like a scary or terrible prison cell at all. Just a regular place, but bigger. I don't want to sound rude or anything so I just keep quiet while Mom and Dad argue about it. When he tells Mom that they're going to get sued by the landlord, she just laughs.

"First they'd have to notice the hole, Russell," she says. "And what's one more in that mess?"

Nanny says you just know they have to be simple in the head or something.

"Perverts. Ignorant perverts. That's what they are. The whole lot of them!"

Up until then, the only other doctor I've ever known is Dr. Burke on Wellington Street, and he's old and bald and I'm not convinced he can even talk. But these young doctors are different. They look dirty, with their messy hair and hippie clothes, but they actually smell okay and smile and talk and ask you how you're doing. Then actually listen when you answer. Everything they say always sounds so…deep. Like it should be printed across the front of a T-shirt or something.

"I'm only an extension of your needs at this moment in time."

They make everything sound like a question, asking for permission to do anything and everything before they do it.

"Do you think it would be okay for me to listen to your heart? Do you think that's an animal bite? Can you tell me if that hurts? How about if we clean that with some of this and then we'll wrap it up with this. Is that okay with you?"

I try not to roll my eyes when one of them says, "You can call me Dr. Turner, Dr. Paul, or even just Paul."

My dad hates them. He says they aren't even real doctors. These ones talk too much, ask too many questions, and try to pretend they're just like us or something. Like that's a good thing. He also hates the other hippies that Mom has started hanging around with, telling her they're all troublemakers and commies just trying to rile people up for nothing.

"At least they care about what happens to me and your kids," she says. "At least they're around and trying to help us change stuff."

That shut my dad up. Until the feminists moved in and, according to my dad, put my mom's head on backwards.

"Those dykes are just going to mix you all up! You need your head screwed back on."

When he went away again I knew it was Mom's fault. She's always complaining about everything, making it sound like it's his fault that we don't have food all the time, like she just wants to make him feel bad. My dad also hates how dirty our place always is.

"I'm not used to living like this!" he says.

Mom laughs, but in a mean way, and then says yes, he's more used to living with his mother. She says the word 'mother' like she's saying "dog shit."

But why wouldn't my dad prefer to live at Nanny's place, where everything is nice and tidy and has its place? At Nanny's there's always a loaf of Weston bread and a butter dish parked in the middle of the kitchen table, with a pot of tea always boiling on the stove and a sack of Redpath sugar in the small cabinet next to the fridge with a tin of Carnation condensed milk. Why wouldn't he leave us? But sometimes me and my sisters can't help it and try to convince him to stay, promising to keep the place cleaner.

"I swear Dad, we'll take turns, honest! Ruth will clean the kitchen every single day, Annie will sweep everywhere, I'm gonna..."

But he leaves anyway, usually to move in with Nanny. Then we all go back to wiping the crumbs off our feet before slipping into bed each night.

We haven't had supper for three days now. I finally decide to remind Mom, just in case she's forgotten about it, and instead of getting mad at me she picks up the phone. Nanny shows up a little while later. At first I thought she had some food for us, but then I see she has some shirts for Dad hanging over her arm.

"Are you sure you haven't seen him?" Mom asks when she sees the shirts. "I haven't seen him in days. When you see him, tell him his kids are hungry."

Nanny's mouth becomes a thin, almost invisible line. You can tell she's angry when her mouth disappears. She doesn't say anything to Mom, though. Maybe it's because it's hard to talk when her mouth is all scrunched up like that.

"They haven't eaten in days," Mom says. "Do you have any eggs or bread I can borrow?"

Nanny manages to open her mouth, but it sounds like each word takes a lot of effort. "I have nothing to spare."

Mom is quiet for a moment. "Ruth is hungry too," she finally says. She knows Ruth is Nanny's favourite.

"Then send her over," Nanny says.

I admit my mom is usually calmer with Dad gone, even if she's always busy. Instead of the loud arguments with my dad each night, she sits at the kitchen table with the Outsiders from McGill. The hippies are becoming her best friends as they begin plotting and deciding how they're going to start the Revolution in the Point. I can ask her all kinds of questions now in front of her new friends and instead of getting mad or ignoring me, she smiles like she thinks I'm funny. When I ask her what's for dinner, instead of her usual "shit on a stick," she says, "Maybe some hot dogs later." You know, pretending like we're normal or something in front of the hippies. I think they make my mom feel like she's famous the way they hang off her every word. The more she complains about the rats and roaches, the happier they seem. When she stands up and moves the Royal Bank calendar on the kitchen wall, showing one of the roaches' favourite hiding places, her new friends all jump like they think roaches can fly. One of them says they'll bring a camera next time. What kind of pervert wants to take a picture of roaches? I can hardly wait to tell Nanny about that part.

"You are making that up!" she says, using the voice that means she's praying to the Lord that I'm not.

"I swear Nanny, it's the truth. I think he's going to give them to *The Star*. Seth said he knows someone there who likes that kind of stuff."

After Nanny says my mom must be sick in the head to be allowing perverts and commies like that in our apartment, I tell her I'm just kidding, that of course no one really wants to be taking pictures of some roaches. Doesn't she know a joke when she hears one? She tells me to go home, saying she doesn't want any little liars in her house. I quickly distract her since I haven't had any toast yet.

"One of them, her name is Belinda, doesn't even wear a bra and I swear Nanny, I'm not kidding now, the boys at the park were all looking down her top when she was bent over, filling out some papers for us to all sign our names on!"

I have her now. But I've saved the best part for last.

"And after I whispered to her that the boys were all looking down her shirt whenever she bent over, you know what she said?" Nanny shakes her head.

"Nothing! She just smiled at me then went right back to what she was doing!"

Belinda is going to hell. That's for sure. She'll probably be right next to those astronauts that Nanny says God is going to punish for thinking they can fly right by Heaven like they did, just a couple of weeks before Halloween. I know not to make the joke me and my sisters keep making about whether or not they'll be able to trick-or-treat while they're up there.

"The Americans are going to suffer His wrath for daring to believe they could send simple men to muck and play among the Heavens. You mark my words!"

When my mom tells her new friends at the next kitchen meeting about the cars racing up and down the streets, and then asks me to tell them about that car that hit me on Charlevoix Street that time and then went racing off before even checking to see if I was dead or not, I say I can't remember. Mom glares at me for a second and then one of her new friends changes the subject.

"Oh yes, Eileen, you're absolutely right. The city of Montréal has abandoned you and your children and we need to get their attention."

I'm glad Mom seems to see now that it's the city of Montréal that has left us all alone. Not my dad. It's the city's fault that the paint on the windowsills has lead in them. Ruth is the best at peeling huge strips off. I carefully bite through the crispy sweet chips with my front teeth, hoping I won't have to share with the two youngest when I get a really nice piece off in one shot.

The hippies tell our mom that it's time to fight, time to be heard.

"We use whatever tools are available to us," they explain.

A few days later, when our mom tells us to lie down on the street, we quickly pick a spot that looks free of dog shit and small rocks. As the oldest, Ruth gets to lie down first, then motions for the rest of us to follow. We clench our eyes shut as our mom spray-paints across our chests, "20 MILES PER HOUR!" Our faces now salted with tiny specks of stray orange paint, the crooked capital 'M' on my chest feels heavy. Mom puts down the can of paint and picks up her bullhorn. I wonder where in the hell she got that from. Probably one of the feminists. They always have shit like that. That, and clip boards.

"Tweny miles an hour! Twenty miles an hour! TWENTY MILES AN HOUR!" she shrieks at each passing car.

Some drivers slow down, leaning forward in their seats as if to get a closer look at the breathing carpet of children lying on the ground. Ruth gives me an angry poke after I give the finger to a man who yells, "Stupid assholes!" out his car window. My mom tightly patrols our bodies, blocking traffic, while she shrieks into her bullhorn. "TWENTY MILES AN HOUR!" I'm worried she's going to get run down if she doesn't get out of the way. But she stands her ground, forcing the cars to go around her, shaking a fist at the ones that drive by so fast, they must have not noticed the crowd of chanting mothers and giggling kids lying in the middle of the road. A few shake their heads as they speed by, just inches from the crowd of mothers trying to slow traffic down. I wonder if any of the passing cars is the one that hit Bobbie Mitchell last week, sending him to the hospital. Or maybe the car that had hit and killed Sandy Vickers. I wonder if our mothers would drag the driver out of his car if they knew which one he was, and what they would do to him. But mostly I think about how glad I am to be skipping school.

In the Montréal *Gazette* the next day there's a picture of Sarah Gauthier looking like a crazy person, waving her bullhorn around with a real mad look on her face.

"Why didn't the photographer run the picture of the kids?" asks my mom. "Wouldn't that have been a better picture?"

Her new friends explain that next time they'll make sure to call the right reporter. I didn't know there's a right and a wrong reporter. I wonder how you can tell them apart.

Seth, the hippie with the short beard that at first made me think he was a hundred, suddenly asks us kids what our favourite kind of cake is. It's like we've all been struck mute. What a weird question. Rich people don't know how to do normal small talk. For a couple seconds I can't even think straight. A favourite cake?

"I dunno. You mean like a May West or Joe Louis?"

"No, that's a single serving," explains Seth.

Single serving? I roll those words around in my head. Single means one. Serving means…giving it to someone? Making their bed? Giving a blowjob? What does any of that have to do with cake? A favourite cake? Seth is talking again. The other hippies are listening now too, grinning and nodding their heads.

"I mean like a family-sized cake."

Oh. Like on TV.

"Like the Banquet Cake they sell at the dépanneur?" asks Ruth.

Thank god for Ruth. She's always good like that. She knows what to say when people aren't making any sense or asking impossible questions or just being weird in some way.

"That long skinny one with the hard icing?" continues Ruth.

"I guess that one. That's the one we always get for the family." Ruth is almost as good at lying as I am. She always knows what to say.

We pretend not to know what it means when Seth gets up and leaves the apartment. But once he's gone, we all rush to the kitchen, trying to lay dibs on the forks. With my luck I'll end up with the bent one or the one with that black spot we can't get off no matter how much we try. Annie picks one out for Hannah and Beth, the two youngest, saying fair is fair. Me and Julia both reach for the same one but Ruth scoops it outta our reach, saying "Thanks!" Ah fuck. I'm going to have to use a damn spoon. I try getting Hannah to trade but Annie tells me to stop being mean and leave her alone with her fork. How is it mean if a three-year-old is just as happy to use a spoon? Before I even ask Beth to trade, she's offering it up to me. But Annie shakes her head and I have to tell Beth, even though she's four, no thanks. Everyone gets to keep their stupid forks.

When Seth gets back with the cake, we pretend not to notice. You know, to be polite and all. Rich people get anxious if they think you're feeling nervous or anxious yourself about anything. Instead we silently track his movements around the room, wondering when he's ever going to admit he bought the cake. Finally.

"Is this the one?" he asks, a proud grin on his face.

Yawn. A cake? Oh, okay. Right, a cake.

"Oh, yeah, right. Uh, thanks. I guess." I instantly feel bad about how sad he looks.

"You got the exact right one," Ruth quickly adds. "Really, we love it so much we're gonna buy ten of them when we win the Super Lotto."

When he pulls out a small package of plastic forks, I wonder where he bought them. Does Duffy's Variety at the corner sell plastic forks? He hands them out like he's giving us each a balloon.

"And one for you and one for you!"

He even has a plastic knife to cut the cake.

His eyebrows go up as he watches my sister Annie cut the cake into eleven perfect pieces. But Annie is fair like that. Eleven people in the house. Eleven pieces of cake. Fair is fair. Annie is always in charge of stuff like that. Ruth would have given bigger pieces to the grownups. I would have tried to rip off Hannah with a smaller piece than the rest of us since she'd never notice anyway. But not Annie. Somehow without using a ruler she always manages to make everything all equal and fair. When Seth takes just a tiny bite of his cake, I give my sisters the "look." Dibs. Of course, Annie will cut it into six perfect tiny pieces later, but I have to try.

Seth eats his slice of cake like it's a chip of paint from the windowsill, using only his front teeth. When he finishes the part he wanted to eat and puts the other half down, he seems as proud as if he just forced down some dog shit or something.

"Well that's the end of that!"

I debate whether to clap my hands, then decide my mom would kill me so I just pretend not to notice. Asshole. After they leave, I break my fork into a pile of tiny pieces.

When the med school students from McGill went door to door in the Point, asking people, "Do you think you need a community-based health care clinic?" everyone thought they were nuts. I mean, who would say no? Some people thought it was a trick question. Like somehow answering it would give away what they were doing with their welfare cheque. When they got to Nanny's place on Liverpool Street, she slammed the door in their faces, muttering about faggots and freaks burning in hell right along with the Devil's own imps. Within a few weeks of the clinic opening, everyone is calling it "that Communist place." But we all go anyway. Our mothers make us. The nurses explained to all the mothers how they're entitled to an extra ten dollars a month from the welfare office for food. The nurses are smarter than they look. The social worker explains to my mom how she can become a welfare advocate.

"With someone as articulate and compassionate and knowledgeable as you are, Mrs. Dobson..."

If she had paws, Mom would have licked them and washed her face with them right on the spot.

"That's just stupid," says my dad. "Why would you want to get yourself into trouble for other people? Calling it a "welfare advocate" is just their way of trying to make you think you're important or something. A welfare advocate just means telling the whole world that you're on welfare. That, and a card carrying official pain-in-the-ass. These people are just using you, Eileen. You know that, right?"

I don't think Mom agrees.

"Not everyone thinks I'm stupid, you know. You think I don't know why those crazy bitches come looking for you here, Russell? I mean, THEY might think I'm stupid..."

If she had just stopped talking right then and there after Dad told her to stop flapping her lips, nothing else would have happened. Ruth made us all go into the bedroom. When I peeked through the crack, I saw Mom sitting on a chair in the middle of the room, her head down, with Dad moving around her like a big dog.

"Sometimes you just talk too much, you know that? You need to learn when to shut your big mouth."

Ruth pulled me away from the crack.

"Stop being such a troublemaker!" she hissed in my ear.

When one of the workers down at the welfare office was mean

to a mother from Ryde Street, talking to her like she was a shop-lifter or something when she had only been trying to get a pair of glasses for her son, my mom spent the whole morning on the phone calling everyone she knew. Her hippie friends taught her months ago that she needed to make lists of everyone.

"There's no need to humiliate someone who is just exercising their legal right to financial aid. These glasses are for her seven-year-old son. He can't see a thing without them! We need to make ourselves be heard..."

Dad says that Mom's new friends have given her too many big words to throw around and it's only going to get her into a lot of trouble. The next morning, my mom is sitting on the floor in the hallway at the welfare office with about twenty other mothers and most of us kids. Two of her new friends are sitting on the floor with us, telling us to stay calm and be polite. Which means no fuck-yous or fuck-offs while we're here.

"It just dilutes the message."

My mom's newest friend, Pierre, is the first French person I can watch up close and know he's not going to call me a blockhead. Mom warned us to stop saying Pepper and Frog and Frenchie. I want to ask her what we're supposed to call them now but I can't think of how to ask the question without sounding rude. Then I hear Seth call them "francophones" and I wonder why calling them a French phone is okay, or better than calling them a Frog? When I tell Ruth and Annie that Pierre is a frankiephone, they warn me not to let Mom hear me talk like that. I try explaining that's what Seth called Pierre but my sisters tell me it's like a coloured person calling another coloured person a nigger.

"But Seth isn't a coloured person."

"No, but he's a rich person," Ruth explains. Oh.

For the first hour or so in the welfare office it's strangely quiet. The workers all ignore us, pretending not to notice that the hallway is so stuffed, the only way you can get past us is to lean against the wall with your hands, stepping carefully over the sea of legs and heads. Then someone gives my mom a nod and she begins to sing.

"Think of your fellow man, lend him a helping hand. Put a little love in your heart..."

My mom actually has a pretty good voice, though I cringe every time she lets loose at home, something she does a lot while sweeping the kitchen floor or hanging out the laundry. God she's embarrassing. Everyone else is frozen, as if surprised to hear her singing. At first she sings alone, then some of the other mothers join her when she gets to the part about;

"Another day goes by... and still the children cry. Put a little love in your heart...and the world will be a better place, and the world will be a better place, for you and me, you just wait and see..."

Our singing seems to bug the shit out of the welfare workers, finally pushing them over the edge. We ignore their glares. When one of them yells at us to shut the hell up, "*maudits Anglais!*" we just sing louder. We're still singing,

"If you want the world to know...we won't let hatred grow put a little love in your heart...And the world will be a better place," when the police show up.

When they demand to know who's in charge, my mom sings out, "You just wait... and see!" making everyone laugh.

She's never looked happier. The Revolution has begun.

Chapter Two

My Uncle Patrick always keeps a gun taped under his kitchen table and mirrors set up on the balcony to help him keep an eye on the back entrance to his apartment. I don't know who he's worried about sneaking up behind him but he never worries about the front because you have to be buzzed in. Mom always laughs and says his security is just stupid.

"He's in city housing for Christ sake. All kinds of riff-raff go in and out of that building day and night."

Uncle Patrick's apartment building is one of the first the city put up in the Point. We were so jealous that he and Aunt Olive and their kids get to live in one before we did. Mom always says it's unfair since Uncle Patrick only has three kids and we have six.

"I'd like to know whose dick he sucked."

Dad says Uncle Patrick just spoke to the right people. If Mom had asked him nicely to tell her the names of some of those people instead of always saying nasty stuff about him, maybe we would have got our own apartment a whole lot sooner. City housing in the Point is pretty fancy. Everything is new and they even give you a brand new fridge and stove when you first move in. Mom says it's like winning the lottery. The floors are all flat, the paint won't make you sick, and the pipes give you hot and cold water. And it takes almost two years before the roaches find the place and move in, but even then, the city pays for some guys in orange overalls and face masks to show up every couple of months to spray the shit out of the place and, according to Nanny, send them back to hell. Until they escape from hell again and come back. Uncle Patrick's rent even includes the heating so he gets to sweat all winter with the windows wide open to let in the fresh air. Nanny says leaving windows open in the winter is a sin and just showing off but Mom says Uncle Patrick is telling the city to go fuck itself by not having to put those big sheets of plastic on his windows anymore like the rest of us each winter. I'm not sure how being able to see out every window in his apartment in the winter is telling the city to fuck off but I know Mom likes that about Uncle Patrick, even if she acts like he's an idiot most of the time.

But I'm not surprised Uncle Patrick tells the city to go fuck itself. He's isn't afraid of anything or anyone and even Mom knows that. He's my favourite uncle and not just because he isn't a perv. He's the only uncle I'm not afraid of ever. He lets me come over any time I want to and as long as I'm quiet, he usually lets me sit in the kitchen for as long as I want. Sometimes he looks at me and tells me to go see Aunt Olive but he only does that when he has to do business and he doesn't want the guys he has coming in the kitchen looking at me.

"I might have to shoot them," he says with a laugh. I'm pretty sure he's just joking.

Mom keeps saying the city is going to kick Uncle Patrick and his family out because of all the improvements he's always making but that doesn't make any sense. Uncle Patrick and Aunt Olive made the place even better after they moved in. Aunt Olive got rid of the city's barf green on all the walls and made the kitchen a dark orange, even all the cupboards. Mom says it's like Halloween in there year round. And Uncle Patrick had some guys cut a hole in the wall between the kitchen and small bedroom. That way he can pass stuff through the wall and just drop it on the floor without ever having to leave the kitchen. Aunt Olive knows to run and pick it all up as soon as she hears the sound of stuff hitting the floor, and like Uncle Patrick says, the beauty of it is that nobody standing in the kitchen can even see her unless they lean across Uncle Patrick and peek behind the small curtain he has hanging there. Nobody is going to lean across Uncle Patrick.

My friend Holly's father has a gun too but I don't think he ever worries about anyone sneaking up on him, because his isn't taped under the kitchen table. It's up on a shelf and Holly told me there aren't even any bullets in it. Her father keeps them separate, in a small box up on a different shelf.

Uncle Patrick says having an unloaded gun up on a shelf is just the same as having no gun at all.

Holly has a different idea about the gun. She says that if her father gets really mad at somebody, like Holly's mother, he'll have time to think about it and cool down when he goes to get the bullets.

Whenever we go over to Uncle Patrick's place, me and my sisters always go through the back by the balcony. We know to wave at Uncle Patrick's mirrors as we push open the big glass sliding door and step right into the kitchen. Mom always says Uncle Patrick lives in that kitchen but I would too if I could. His kitchen is always warm and there's always something to eat and lots of tea to drink with a tin of Carnation milk always ready on the counter. Uncle Patrick doesn't like to keep it in the fridge because it cools down the tea. Aunt Olive keeps saying he's going to get poisoned when the tin turns funny from sitting out on the counter all the time but I always think it tastes okay. Some days Uncle Patrick won't have any visitors and he'll sit at the table loading and unloading his gun, holding it up to the light and staring up the barrel, like he's trying to look for something hidden inside. I think it's a kind of game he likes to play. Instead of hopscotch or elastics, he loads and unloads that gun. Mom says he just has shit for brains and is going to blow his own face off one day.

Only one person has ever made it to Uncle Patrick's gun before he has. Aunt Olive was lying on the sofa in the living room when little Calvin, the kid she babysits from next door, waddled into the room and clunked her on the head with something hard.

"Fuck me!" says Aunt Olive.

She looks up and there's little Calvin, pointing Uncle Patrick's gun at her. She screamed so loud she scared the shit out of him and he dropped the gun. Uncle Patrick came out of the bathroom and when he saw what had happened, he laughed so hard he had to hang onto the wall until he finished.

Dad doesn't keep any guns at our place when he lives with us.

I don't think he worries about us touching it or anything. I think he's afraid Mom will try and shoot him again. He likes to tell the story sometimes after he comes home from the Legion. He could tell it a million times and it would still always make him laugh.

"I'm in a dead sleep yet something, somehow, wakes me up on a dime. I open one eye and sure enough, there's Eileen standing over me with my police revolver in her right hand, pointed right at my face."

Unlike Holly's father, my dad's bullets weren't in a little box on a different shelf. They were inside the gun. Dad grins at the memory of Mom holding the loaded gun just inches from his nose. He can see her hand is shaking a bit. She's crying.

"I've never felt more alive than I did at that moment. Her hand is trembling, the tears are rolling down her face, and I know she's just seconds away from blowing my brains out all over the bed."

That's when Dad starts begging.

"Eileen, what are you doing? You know you're the only one that matters…the only one that has ever mattered. The rest of them are just bullshit, nobodies, just pieces of ass for a quick…"

"SHUT UP!" screams Mom, right in his face. "Just SHUT UP."

Then Mom starts to cry again and Dad can see her finger twitching. Before she can yell at him again he suddenly reaches up and slaps the gun right out of her hand.

Dad says from then on he always took a shower before coming to visit Mom. I think it's mean to want to shoot somebody's face off just because you don't like the way they smell. And I don't think it's funny that Mom almost shot Dad's face off. Uncle Patrick and Dad think gun stuff is funny, I guess.

Mom says Uncle Patrick should be more worried about the shit going on all around him, right under his own nose, instead of parking his big ass at the kitchen table all day. Dad dares her to say his brother has a big ass again and Mom just laughs, and then says she was wrong. Uncle Patrick has a huge ass. I think that was kind of mean of her. Dad says Uncle Patrick wasn't always that big and fat.

"He was a real looker and could have had any woman he wanted; they just loved him, all of them. He dated some of the best looking girls, from some of the most well-connected and important families in Gaspé. Even their fathers loved him."

Dad says Uncle Patrick even used to read books.

"He was a self-educated man. He used to love to argue ideas and make you really think about all kinds of things. We all knew he was going to be a somebody. He was going to be famous. Maybe even change the world."

Dad always says stuff like that about Uncle Patrick after he's had a few. To his face, he just jokes and makes him laugh and talks about the old times.

"Pat, remember old Ralph, that guy…"

Dad doesn't have to finish the story. They talk like that at each other for hours. Each saying just a few words that make the other laugh. Sometimes Uncle Patrick suddenly sits up in his chair and nods at the mirror with his head.

"Russ, take a look."

And after seeing what Uncle Patrick sees coming up the back driveway, Dad moves from the chair closest to the sliding doors and sits further back in the kitchen. If he has time, he grabs me by the arm and we both leave the kitchen until Uncle Patrick finishes his business.

All kinds of people are always coming in and out of Uncle Patrick's kitchen every day. He says the small table across from his TV is his perch for keeping an eye on things, and I guess he never has to leave the perch since everyone comes and sees him. Mom says they're carrying hot goods, and lots of times they ask Uncle Patrick how to fix stuff, too.

"It's a real mess Pat," says Mr. Browne. He lives a couple of blocks away. He's standing in the doorway waiting for Uncle Patrick to wave him in the rest of the way.

"I know I can't move anything unless you decide you're willing to help me."

Uncle Patrick turns around and sees me pretending to read my book.

"Go see Aunt Olive, okay?" he says and with a nod from my dad, I leave the kitchen.

Along with the gun taped under the table, Uncle Patrick keeps a small notebook and a pen at his perch. He uses it to win all kinds of prizes on *The Price is Right*. Uncle Patrick whips out the notebook when Bob Barker says "A fabulous prize could be yours if the Price is Right!"

Uncle Patrick nearly always knows the price. His notebook has the name and price of every fridge and stove and dishwasher and car they sell in the States.

"I want you to see the first item up for bid right now on *The Price is Right*," Bob Barker is saying.

We both look at the small TV across from Uncle Patrick's perch. It's one of those boring prizes that nobody really wants to win. Uncle Patrick always says the contestant who makes it up on stage and gets stuck bidding on something stupid like that must always feel ripped off.

"We have a new outdoor play set!" says Bob Barker like he's desperate to win it himself.

"For your children's enjoyment, this challenging custom-made play structure features a play house climber, durable slide, monkey bars, a tire swing and a glider for two!"

It definitely doesn't look like the play structure at Ash Park. The slide Bob Barker is showing off doesn't have "COCK SUCKER" spray painted on the front, and there aren't any older girls smoking by the swings. Instead there's a smiling lady in a pink dress, sitting on the tire swing and tossing her hair as the contestants make their bids. Bob Barker tells them the retail price is rounded off to the nearest dollar.

Uncle Patrick flips through his book. Every page is filled with lists of prices: ovens, toasters, a Delsey luggage collection, a red cedar garden trellis, and a jukebox.

"1,220 dollars! 1,220 dollars!" Uncle Patrick calls out when he finds the price in his notebook. He snorts when Heather bids $450. "What the hell's she smoking?"

Julie has the closest bid at $1100, but she shouldn't feel so smug. Uncle Patrick got the exact price and he was a lot faster than her. I bet he'd be even better than Bob Barker. I keep telling him he should go on *The Price is Right*, that he'd win everything.

"I don't think they'd let me bring this," Uncle Patrick says, holding up his notebook.

Mom doesn't like us girls going over to Uncle Patrick's place without Dad. I tell her I'm not dumb, that I'd never touch a gun. Dad already made me promise not to. But Mom says it's not just the guns.

"God knows what kind of idiots he has hanging around there and I don't need you there when he gets raided or busted. I also don't want you or your sisters to see him beating the crap out of Aunt Olive. It's not nice!"

I try telling Mom we don't see Uncle Patrick when he's beating on Aunt Olive. He always makes her leave the room and beats her upstairs. He comes in the room, pulls his belt off and Aunt Olive runs. Their kids turn up the TV in the living room and we all just pretend we don't hear anything.

My friend Helen Brennan's father never cares who's around when he blows his gasket and decides it's time to teach Helen's mom a lesson. I know to just jump out of his way and huddle with Helen behind the daybed in the kitchen.

"You useless piece of shit. You fucking whore!" Mr. Brennan says as he runs at her.

Sometimes she makes it out of the room but most of the time he gets her by the back of her hair or grabs a piece of her shirt and drags her back into the kitchen.

"You fucking cunt. How many times do I have to tell you what the fuck is up? Are you just FUCKING STUPID?"

Helen tells me that her mom knows to just shut up and it'll all be over faster, but sometimes I guess she can't help herself. She tries to explain, maybe hoping this time Mr. Brennan will understand that she didn't mean to make him so mad, and stop beating on her.

31

"Please, Willie, I swear it wasn't like that. I told that worker I didn't know nothing about anything but she said the file is..."

Sometimes Mrs. Brennan's words just make him madder. One time, when he started kicking her she fell to the floor and slowly started to crawl away. When she nearly made it to the door, I looked away and stared at Helen instead. She had her eyes closed so tight the tears were trapped in her lower eyelashes. When I reached out for her hand she opened her eyes and slapped my hand away.

"Fuck you," she said angrily. "FUCK YOU!"

Dad says Uncle Patrick married Aunt Olive by mistake. I think that's maybe why Uncle Patrick hits her—he's still mad at her for tricking him.

"He just woke up one morning and there she was lying next to him," says Dad. "Pat pushed her out of the bed, saying her father would kill them both. Olive had to go and get the marriage certificate to prove it to him."

But I know Uncle Patrick loves Aunt Olive no matter how much he beats her. One Christmas, he bought her a real fur coat. Aunt Olive is so proud of that coat, she's always telling everybody to go ahead and touch it. I let her show it to me all the time. I know it makes her so happy to brag about it.

"Feel it. Really, go ahead. Feel it. That is 100 percent real rabbit fur!"

And the coat really is so nice and soft. It must have taken about a billion bunnies to make it and all of them different colours too. That coat has brown and black and white and even some red. I've never seen a red bunny before, but I sure want to one day. I've never seen any bunny for real in person yet. But Mom tells me it isn't made of real rabbits.

"That coat is 100 percent real Point St. Charles cat fur."

I'm not sure though. I've lived in the Point my whole life and have never seen a red cat once. But this one time when we lived on Charlevoix Street I saw a cat that was a kind of orange colour. I was sitting on one of the bunk beds in the basement and the cat walked up to one of the windows that were on level with the sidewalk, purring softly.

"Here, kitty, kitty," I leaned in close to the screen.

Without any warning the cat suddenly hissed and scratched at the screen, acting like it wanted to rip my throat out if it could only get into the basement somehow. It startled me so much I shouted "Fuck you!" and punched the screen. The cat jumped back and ran off. Annie saw the whole thing and I worried she would think I was some kind of a psycho for trying to punch a cat. Even if it was a crazy one and it startled me.

"What the hell was that about!" she says.

"That fucker wanted to hurt me and all I wanted to do was pet the thing!"

"Do you have any idea how much disease and filth is on one of those things?" says Annie.

"It's a fucking cat," I say.

I mean, how much stuff could be on it anyway?

"You should have kicked it!" says Annie and we both laugh.

Annie tells each and every sister about me trying to beat up a cat, making them laugh when she gets to the part about me trying to punch it.

"After it does this big hiss thing at her, Kathy's feet aren't even touching the ground when she flies up and punches the screen."

Ruth asks if I ripped the screen. "Mom will kill you."

Annie and I roll our eyes behind her bossy-face back. I'm glad Annie didn't think I was mean. The next day she kept making a hissing sound, then throwing a punch in the air, trying to make me laugh about it again.

Mom always says Aunt Olive caught the smacking disease from Uncle Patrick. Their son Marvin would be crying in his crib while Uncle Patrick gave Aunt Olive the belt. Then when he was finished, Aunt Olive would go in and beat baby Marvin. One time Mom got so fed up, she grabbed Aunt Olive by the throat.

"Hit him again you bitch and I swear to god, I'll fucking kill you. Do you hear me? I'll fucking kill you."

Uncle Patrick thinks Mom is the best mother in the whole wide world. When Aunt Olive told him what Mom had done, he smacked Aunt Olive across the face.

"What kind of a mother are you, anyway, beating up your own baby? Eileen's right, you sick bitch. You hit our son again and I'll kill you!"

Aunt Olive didn't hit Marvin when he was a baby anymore after that. Well, not when my mom or Uncle Patrick were around. Now that he's older, Aunt Olive isn't the only one who beats the crap out of him. Every single Halloween, Marvin gets beaten up and his candy stolen. Nobody wants to go trick-or-treating with him anymore. He's just bad luck. He always begs us not to tell his father about being robbed. I thought he was afraid Uncle Patrick would kill the kids who hurt him but Mom told me that no, Marvin knows his father would beat him up for letting those other kids kick the shit out of him.

When Mom told Dad that his brother had tried to get into bed with her, Dad laughed. I thought it was pretty funny that Uncle Patrick would have got in the wrong bed, too.

"You aren't supposed to feel proud that your own brother tried to fuck me," said Mom.

Dad got so mad at her when she said that. He hates it when Mom swears and she swears all the time. It's always fuck this and fuck that. Dad says she doesn't even know when she's swearing anymore.

"You have the filthiest mouth of any woman I've ever known!" Dad says. "How can someone so beautiful have such a dirty mouth?"

When Dad asked Uncle Patrick about getting mixed up about what bed to sleep in, he just grinned. Then shrugged.

"I had to try, right?"

Him and Dad both laughed. Like Nanny always says, they're best friends.

"My boys are so close, so tight, nothing and nobody is ever going to come between them."

When Mom told Dad he could fuck Aunt Olive anytime he wants to, he didn't laugh. He slammed the door on his way out. Why does Mom always have to swear?

When Mom saw a poster the other day at St. Columba House, she copied down a phone number from the bottom. A group of medical school students from McGill University and a nurse are looking for "Anyone interested in improving the healthcare and education of their children or loved ones in Point St. Charles. Free dental and eye examinations available!"

My mom wants to be an Informed Citizen. She has to go to a meeting first to get the free stuff. My dad is back again. He laughs and tells her there's always a catch, that nothing is ever really free. He says they're a bunch of lesbians and commies and feminists. Mom ignores him though. He doesn't stay long.

When Mom comes back from her meeting with the lesbians, commies and feminists she's all excited. She says she got us appointments to see a dentist for free. Mom doesn't laugh when I say the dentist should pay us for going to him. How is letting someone hurt you for free a good thing? Who wants to be a dentist when they grow up, anyway?

"Freaks, " says Annie. "Only a freak would want to sniff shitty breath and pick crap outta stinky mouths all day on purpose."

Annie laughs when I say maybe they should make bad people in jail dentists.

"Shit, now we gotta brush our teeth!" says Annie.

Then she shows me how to wipe my teeth with the corner of a wet towel. I finally know her secret. Annie is the cleanest one in our family and always smells so nice. When we went to Camp Amy Molson for three weeks during the summer she came back with a sunburn, a whole pile of extra clothing, and a can of Lysol Spray that she used to clean the kitchen and bathroom with until every last drop was gone. A lot of the kids from the Point go to Camp Amy Molson every summer but only Annie would steal something as dumb as a can of cleaning shit.

"It was industrial strength!" she says.

Mom worried for a while that maybe the camp social worker would show up or something once we got home. Maybe to get the can of cleaner back, I guess.

"You kids talk too much," says Mom.

But that isn't true. We know never to answer the phone, never to open the door to the Jew, or any guys wearing vests. And if anybody asks if our dad lives with us, we know to say "Nope. Haven't seen him in years."

One time the camp director Mrs. Rogers came over but we hid the can when she was here. Me and Annie tried to listen in as she talked to Mom but she didn't say anything about the missing cleaner.

When the camp bus drove by a bunch of cows in a field last summer I tried to figure out a way to take one home. There were a whole bunch and they weren't tied down or anything. I thought about maybe finding a rope somewhere but didn't know how to get the cow down the highway back to the Point. That would have been something, though. A whole cow just for us. It would have been fun to stick it in the back yard and tell the landlord it's a pet if he bitched at Mom about it. But Annie says cow shit is especially stinky and is a Serious Health Hazard. I'm not sure. I can't totally give up on the idea. I might try to figure out a way to get one of those free cows home next summer. Spencer told me that all you have to do is knock it out with a good whack to the forehead and then you can eat it.

The free dentist doesn't like my sister Beth very much. She keeps moving around in the chair and crying and saying she doesn't want him to look in her mouth.

He says that maybe she has something secret inside she doesn't want him to see, and then gets mad because nobody laughs at his joke.

"You know what?" he says, "You win. I'm done."

Then he won't work on her anymore, even though Mom tries pleading and begging. She's so mad, I think she hurt Beth's arm a little when she yanked her out of the chair.

I think that dentist just didn't want to work on her mouth anyway, the lazy shithead. Who's mean to a scared five-year-old on purpose? When it's my turn I sit down right away and open my mouth so wide, doesn't the jerk have to tell me to, "Close a little, please."

I think he hates me too because instead of using a toothbrush to clean my teeth like he's supposed to, all he does is use a pointy stick thing to scratch my teeth with. Annie laughs when I tell her and after checking out my teeth, she says, "I think that fucker scratched 'Fuck Head was here' on your front tooth."

I hate the way Mom keeps thanking him the whole time like he's saving our lives or something.

"I think it's wonderful that a professional is willing to donate some of his valuable time to helping…"

I tune the rest out. It just makes me feel sick. The fucker. The free toothbrushes are cool, though. I thought Annie was going to hug me to death when I said she can have mine. Later I show her the extra ones I helped myself to when the shithead was busy letting Mom tell him what a hero he is.

I don't hate the free eye doctor and I don't think he hates us either. He seems to even like his job. We all just pretend not to notice the huge fake eye he has on his desk. Creepy, but I guess eye doctors like eyes so much they want to have one they can play with in between seeing patients. When he says he's going to give us a test I know Annie is all nervous. She's the smartest person I know in the whole wide world but she's one of those people who just don't do tests very well. They just make her too nervous and all her smart stuff goes away or something. I'm happy the eye tests are the kind you can't fail.

"Which line do you see better," the doctor asks. "Can you read to me the smallest letter you can see?"

I'm surprised they don't have interesting stuff for you to read at the eye doctor's office. The lines don't make any sense to me.

"That's so you can't memorize it," Annie explains. "It's so you can't cheat."

Who the fuck cheats on a test like that? Shit. Talk about thinking the whole world is fucked up and filled with assholes.

Beth gets to look at colours and bunnies and stuff so she isn't nervous at all with this doctor. He doesn't give us any free stuff but I'm thrilled when he tells my mom that I'll probably be wearing glasses by the time I turn twelve. How cool is that? My own glasses.

After Mom becomes an Informed Citizen, she starts fighting with the welfare office more and more. Even for other people. There's power in numbers, she says. I've never liked math too much but if it can give me some kind of special powers, maybe I'll try and learn it like Annie.

"You know you're going to have to pay for all this one day, right?" Dad says.

I think he's afraid he'll have to pay for it all once he gets a real job because he hates Mom being at all the meetings she's going to.

"I just want to make sure people get what they're entitled to," Mom says.

"You need to focus more on what this family needs," says Dad.

Mom says she's tired of dropping down on all fours every time a car backfires because Dad's hanging around the wrong people. She asks if he'll come with her to the next meeting.

"If you really want to help your own kids you should come and learn about the huge difference between the quality of education your children are getting and the kids in Westmount. Our inner-city kids get screwed from every side."

My dad shakes his head and tells Mom she's being a fool. A fool wasting her time.

"I can't believe you're falling for all that BS. These are social workers you're listening to. You know that, right?"

"Coming from you, that's a joke," says Mom. "At least the social workers are trying to help, are trying to get your kids fed and at least are around. Are you going to buy them fucking underwear? Maybe some socks or a fucking piece of bread? No, you're a goddamn Dobson, you're too fucking important and proud to ask for help even if it is for your own kids. You'd rather let them fucking starve and freeze to death just as long as you have Mommy to run home to, of course, to make sure you get your goddamn fucking eggs and toast every day and then one of your sluts for a warm bed to lay each night. So FUCK YOU RUSSELL! FUCK YOU!"

I can always tell when my dad is really mad. My mom yells and screams and swears but Dad goes all quiet and chooses each word so carefully you'd think he's paying a dime for each and every one. First he gives a mean short laugh.

"You are such a Richardson, Eileen. Born and bred. Will die one, too."

Mom says stuff about how once your eyes are opened they can't ever be shut again and I wonder if I should let her know she's wrong. But before I can decide what to do, Dad slams the door and he's gone again. Mom combs her hair, makes a quick phone call, then yells to Annie that she'll be back soon.

The only time I ever saw Uncle Patrick get mad at my mom is when he found out she was trying to get Aunt Olive to join one of her groups.

"You don't have to live like this," Mom says to Aunt Olive.

They're sitting in the living room drinking some tea. Mom is speaking so softly, I have to lean over to hear what they're saying.

"You don't know him like I do," says Aunt Olive.

I'm waiting for Mom to explain what's wrong with the way Aunt Olive is living. Why she doesn't have to live that way, like Mom said.

"I know him better than you think," says Mom. "I know all about his kind. Don't forget, I'm married to his goddamn brother."

"Russ don't beat on you or the kids," says Aunt Olive. "Or does he?"

Now she looks more awake. She moves to the edge of the couch and looks closely at Mom. Before Mom can say a word, the kitchen door opens and Uncle Patrick walks in the living room.

"Hey Eileen, I didn't know you were here! How'd you get in?"

Uncle Patrick looks at Aunt Olive, then back at my mom and the smile dies on his face.

"Are you filling her head with more bullshit?"

Mom stands up. I wish she was more afraid of Uncle Patrick. I go over and stand next to her.

"Maybe you need to leave." Uncle Patrick says it quietly. I hope Mom is paying attention.

39

"She wasn't saying nothing," says Aunt Olive.

Uncle Patrick smiles at her then looks away.

"Do you want to come with me to my place?" asks Mom. She looks at Aunt Olive. "You can come with me right now."

"Like I don't know where you live," says Uncle Patrick with a mean smile. "It's not right for a woman to come between two brothers, Eileen. You might have my brother all pussy whipped but if you pull any of this shit again, I swear, you will…"

"I will what? Are you threatening me, Pat?" says Mom. She gets right up in Uncle Patrick's face.

"You know I'm not afraid of you, right?"

For a second I'm sure Uncle Patrick is going to hurt her. He takes a big breath. He must be counting to ten.

"You need to leave," says Uncle Patrick. "Right now. Go."

I pull on Mom's arm. "Come on, Mom, let's go. Okay? Please?"

This is exactly the kind of stuff people are always saying about my mom in the Point, how she needs more sense about shit like this. Some people say it's my dad's fault. That he needs to teach her better manners and shit. Some people say the Outsiders have crawled up Mom's ass so far, they've started to mess with her brains. But my mom's always been the type to say stuff other people don't always want to hear if she thinks it needs saying. Like that time a thirteen-year-old girl was knocked down in the Wellington tunnel and after the two men finished messing with her, three months later she found out she was pregnant. She'd been crying at the clinic, saying she was going to kill herself if they didn't rip that baby out of her body, but her parents said she couldn't murder their own grandchild and wouldn't sign the papers. When she couldn't find a doctor to give the girl an abortion, Mom helped smuggle her over the border and had an American doctor take care of it. Some people in the Point wouldn't talk to my mom anymore after that, saying she was a baby killer. Mom says those people are just fucking idiots who don't even know they're fucking slaves yet. I hope she doesn't think Uncle Patrick or Aunt Olive are slaves. Or if she does, I hope she doesn't plan on telling them to their faces.

"I'll leave," Mom says to Uncle Patrick. "This is your home."

Mom looks over at Aunt Olive. She's curled up on the couch now. I think she's asleep.

"But Olive, you always know where to find me."

"Don't push your luck, " says Uncle Patrick.

He's holding the front door open. That's how I know he's mad. Real mad. I make sure Mom goes through the doorway first. Uncle Patrick isn't really much of a kicker but you never know. I can tell Mom has pissed him off pretty good.

"Bye Uncle Patrick!" I say.

I guess he can tell I still love him even if he's acting all scary at my mom because he smiles back at me and then winks as he watches us go down the stairs.

"Bye Kathy."

He doesn't say goodbye or anything to my mom though. Once we hit the sidewalk I have to run behind her to stay caught up. Uncle Patrick must have called my dad right away because when we get home, he's leaning against a car in front.

At first I think Mom doesn't see him. She's halfway up the stairs before she says anything.

"You don't have a key for a reason, Russell," says Mom.

"I can't believe you would pull a stunt like that with my own brother. Are you crazy now? Do you know who you're screwing with? Have those feminists made you so…"

Mom is ignoring Dad and still walking up the stairs.

"I'm speaking to you, Eileen," says Dad. "What happened to the woman I married?"

She knows he won't raise his voice outside. Dad is big on keeping family stuff in the family. I'm surprised he's said as much as he has already. He knows the neighbours are all pressed up against the cracks of their front doors or staring out their windows. Mom stops on the steps and turns around.

"She's dead, Russell," she says. "She died a long time ago."

"Don't even think of ever allowing Olive to move in with you," says Dad as Mom continues up the stairs. "You know that can't happen, right?"

Mom laughs and keeps walking. I know why Dad is telling her that, though. Mom is always collecting people to let move in with us. Cousins with missing mothers, kids whose fathers have kicked the shit of them and are now afraid to go back home.

A few nights later a friend of hers arrives at our door in a police cruiser with her two young kids.

"I'm sorry Eileen, " cries Mrs. Collins. "I didn't know what else to do. Where else to go."

The police officer that helps her and the kids into our place explains to Mom that there was a fire over on Knox Street and everything that hasn't burned has been pretty much destroyed by the water when the fire department was fighting the blaze.

"Oh you poor thing," says Mom as she folds Mrs. Collins into her arms. "You'll stay here of course!"

Within a few days the fun of having two extra kids staying with us wears off and we're starting to hope the Collins family will find a new place to stay real soon. Mom calls all the agencies she can think of to get some emergency money for Mrs. Collins but all they ask about is the whereabouts of Mr. Collins and then tell my mom she should try one of the churches. I still thank Mrs. Collins for making Dad come around again, though, after he almost bashed her and my mom's kneecaps one night. Dad heard that someone had moved in with us and one night he snuck in with his baseball bat and crept down the hallway so softly, no one heard a peep. Once he got to Mom's room he saw the two bodies lying in the bed and just as that bat was about to come crashing down, didn't Mrs. Collins move, and Dad, as he laughed and explained later, saw her white bra glowing in the dark. He must have felt bad about it because for the next two weeks he came by almost every single morning for a cup of coffee, sitting at the table with Mom and Mrs. Collins, laughing and smoking Player's. When Mrs. Collins gave birth months later, I guess she must have felt really thankful to Mom and Dad cause didn't she name that little boy "Russell." She had already moved out from our place months and months ago, so I think it was nice of her to remember Mom's act of kindness like that.

Chapter Three

My best friend Jenny Quinn thinks it's weird that my mom never hits me or my sisters. If my Dad were the slapping kind, which he isn't, Mom wouldn't let him hit us either. Jenny didn't believe me at first.

"She won't hit you at all, no matter what?"

No matter what.

"What if you...killed somebody?"

Nope. She knows I'd only kill somebody for a good reason.

"But what if you do something real bad?" Jenny persists. "Like take some of your mom's smokes?"

My mom is pretty clear. "If a teacher ever sends you to the office for the strap, or dares to hit you, come home. Just leave the school and come straight home."

The whole class can hear Spencer Lowry getting the strap down the hall. He's standing in front of the office and crying like a baby while Mr. Doyle, the principal, counts out loud.

"One..." SMACK.

"Two..." SMACK.

"Hold your hand out, boy, or this will just take longer."

Spencer takes four hits before he starts begging.

"Please Sir, I promise never to..."

"HOLD IT OUT!"

We pretend not to listen anymore. When I tell my mom about it later, for a moment I think she's having a heart attack. She holds onto the back of her chair while she reaches for the phone.

"Who you calling, Mom?"

At first I think I've done something bad. Maybe I'm in trouble? But I realize that Mom's calling the school.

"Mr. Doyle, how dare you beat a child...what? You know he

43

isn't my son, but that isn't the point! Just because you have the legal right to abuse your students doesn't mean…"

At first Mr. Doyle tries blowing her off, saying it wasn't her child he had been beating on so why is she being so bossy and stuff about it. But Mom doesn't take any of that crap from him. Mom just can't help herself. Something inside her seems to snap if she hears of anybody beating on any kid. Dad says it's because Mom was raised by a Perverted Bully.

The first time a teacher ever slapped me I was in grade three. I admit it was my own fault. I was leaning over and whispering to Geralyn when Mrs. Tremblay noticed and told me to be quiet. I shut up for a minute but then I forgot and leaned over to whisper that Jamie Moore has donkey ears. Suddenly Mrs. Tremblay was standing behind me. She smacked the top of my head and then whipped around and whacked me across the face with her ruler. I heard the whoosh before it hit my face, but I didn't know I was bleeding until Marsha pointed at me and said, "Your face!"

At first it was like everybody was holding their breath. I touched the wetness on my cheek and then looked at Mrs. Tremblay. I almost felt sorry for her.

"You are so dead."

I moved towards the door to leave, feeling stupid and trying not to cry. The other kids were all staring at me but they were breathing again. Mrs. Tremblay's voice made me jump.

"Sit down!"

I ignored her. I was almost at the door.

"I said SIT DOWN!"

She was suddenly blocking the doorway, now standing in front of me. Her eyes were as black as her long stringy hair.

Geralyn and Marsha and Jenny and Spencer all rushed the door at once.

"Go Kathy, go!"

Jenny shoved Mrs. Tremblay while Spencer pulled on the back of her shirt. Marsha and Geralyn pushed me from behind but suddenly I was being yanked by the back of my head. Mrs. Tremblay had me trapped in her fingers. I climbed her body like a cat and broke free. As I rushed down the hallway I looked down at the long strands of black hair wrapped around my fist. Gross. I didn't have to run home. I knew I could find my mom in the kindergarten class since she goes there every morning and reads stories to the kids. It's the kind of thing Informed Citizens do. But afterwards I wished I had just stayed in the classroom. I didn't mean for Mrs. Tremblay to get in so much trouble. I told Mr. Doyle it didn't even really hurt all that much and the blood looked bad but when I wiped my face it was just a red scratch on my cheek. I pulled Mrs. Tremblay's hair really hard, that's why she pulled mine, too.

After she leaves we get a new teacher that makes us sing French songs all day. My favourite is *L'école est finie* by Sheila. It's on the radio a million times a day.

> *Donne-moi ta main et prends la mienne*
> *La cloche a sonné ça signifie*
> *La rue est à nous que la joie vienne*
> *Mais oui Mais oui l'école est finie*

At Lorne School, being polite is more important than anything else. I mostly get E's for excellent and C's for commendable on my report cards. Same with my sisters, except for Annie, who only gets E's. No need for improvement with Annie at all. Even though I pulled Mrs. Tremblay's hair before she pulled mine, me and my sisters never tell any teacher to go fuck themselves or worse, to go fuck a duck. We never mutter "Asshole" under our breath when the principal or vice principal walks by, even though my mom says the whole Point knows the principal is a major asshole. The vice-principal is okay, though. This one time he stepped outside the school when the Callaghan gang was dicking with a couple of other kids. He didn't wait to figure out exactly who was there or how many there were first. He saw the Callaghan gang being a bunch of shitheads and he just got right in their faces.

"How about you go fuck yourselves!"

I like how if someone is doing something they shouldn't in

the back of the school, he doesn't just stand in the doorway and shout "Hey! Hey! Stop it!" and then quickly run back into the school after getting a couple of hard glares or the finger. He gets right into their faces and tells them to fuck off right back. Mom says that's why the school board hired him to be the vice principal, so he can tell bad kids to fuck off when they need a good fuck off.

I think most of the teachers at the school like me and my sisters. We don't rip any pages out of the books in the library with the librarian looking on, or cut out any pictures from the fancy magazines. We never write shit like, "Mrs. Klein is a fat fucking cunt," on the bathroom walls, or print her phone number with a line about, "Call me tonight for a really hot date." We never put the garbage cans in the bathroom on fire or shove a whole roll of toilet paper down the toilet and then flush. Besides, most of the toilet paper rolls are stuck to the wall, trapped inside one of those metal cases with only a bit of the paper sticking out the bottom. Another kid showed me the pencil trick last year, where you wrap a pencil in the toilet paper and start unrolling it real fast, so you end up with a whole new roll of toilet paper wrapped around the pencil. We bring new pencil rolls home whenever we can. But we never do anything sinful like waste it.

I think most of the teachers at Lorne School are okay, but my mom says some of them are the rejects from the fancy schools around Montréal. Maybe she means Mr. Howard. He's real friendly, especially with the best-looking girls. Sometimes he brings them to the cloakroom during math, saying he needs to see them back there. When I asked Mom after school one day if it was true that if a man had his balls blown off in the war, he'd go crazy because he couldn't have sex anymore, she asked me who had told me that. It hurt my feelings when she didn't believe me and called a whole bunch of other mothers until a few of them, after asking their kids, told her that yeah, Mr. Howard had said that. Mom says teachers like that aren't good enough for the rich kids in Westmount but good enough for Point kids. Sort of like the textbooks. When Mom found out at one of her Informed Citizen's meetings that we use different books from the kids at the schools in Westmount and Outremont and even Verdun, she marched right over to the school.

"These are the same books my husband and I used when we were attending Lorne School!"

Mr. Doyle made the mistake of asking Mom what was wrong with that.

"If they were good enough for you and your husband and your entire generation…"

Mom told him how those nice looking kids, Dick and Jane and Sally, with their cute dog, were all wrong for us Point kids. I wanted to ask Mom what was wrong with them. Maybe they had some kind of infection or bedbugs or something I couldn't tell from looking at the pictures? The mom and dad looked really nice but maybe he was a secret Perverted Bully or something?

Mom told Mr. Doyle that the ripped up books with missing pages and extra shit written inside, like "Jane's dad is a fucking faggot who sucks off his dog," isn't very nice, either. She said that we want new books. With clean pages. Like the rich kids.

"I've taken note of your concerns," said Mr. Doyle.

Mom says that's an educator's polite way of saying 'Fuck off.'

In those Dick, Jane and Sally books the TVs are always sitting in a room with a nice carpet and a couch and a table, sometimes even a lamp. In the Point, if there's a hockey game going on, then there's a TV perched on a chair on the sidewalk in front of almost every building. You can watch the game all the way home, passing from one TV to the next.

"Yvan Cournoyer, moving past the center line… he shoots, he scores!" the announcer says.

Some of the Peppers scream, "*Il lance….. il compte! C'est un buuuuuuuuuuuut!*"

As long as it's the Bruins or Toronto playing against the Canadiens, no one tells the Peppers to "Shut the fuck up!"

Most of the time I don't care much about hockey, but sometimes I have a dime to get in on the pool. Sheila Kelly is the runner who takes the bets, and if there's a penalty or a goal at 10:13 in the second period, that dime becomes ten bucks. I always open my ticket before the game starts and when the time on my piece of paper starts getting close, I try to mentally push the puck into the net or one of the player's sticks under someone else's leg. Uncle Patrick doesn't even touch his tickets until the game is over.

"That would ruin the game," he always says.

For me, opening that ticket is the only way to make the game interesting. Every time there's a goal or a penalty, Uncle Patrick writes it down in his little notebook. When the game ends, he opens his tickets one at a time, holding them up to the notebook and then putting them down on the table in neat little rows. By the time he finishes opening all his tickets, they always cover the whole table.

Those Dick, Jane and Sally books never have TVs on the sidewalks, even during hockey games, but Annie says the stuff the rich kids read is all boring and fake.

"They're always going on trips somewhere, and even the kids have their own sunglasses."

At school the next day, everyone is sitting at their desks. We're tracing the alphabet and I'm making my 'S's so perfectly. Kevin looks out the window and yells, "Incoming Frenchies!" Everybody drops their pencils and pushes back their chairs. The classroom empties in seconds. We rush down the hallway, screaming, "The Peppers are here! THE PEPPERS ARE HERE!" Now the whole school is dropping their pencils and pushing back their chairs, and everyone is in the schoolyard in minutes. One of the French Catholic schools has arrived. We can all barely fit in the yard. Someone yells, "That fucking Frog has a chain!" and I turn and watch as the Pepper swings it in a big circle. One of the grade seven boys knocks him over and takes the chain. He starts to swing it until someone knocks him over and takes their turn until they get knocked over, too. I scan the yard for my sisters. I see Ruth making her way towards me, Annie close behind. When they reach me, they go back to back and shove me in the middle.

I start pointing, "There's a Pepper! There's a Pepper!"

At first the teachers yell at us to get back inside but they know we can't hear them and soon they give up and go back inside alone. My cousin Marvin is having the shit kicked out of him until his younger brother, Bruce, runs at the kicking Pepper with a baseball bat, but some of the older kids take it away from him. Bruce just forgot the rules. Ruth grabs my arm and pulls me towards the brick wall.

"Stay here!" she commands.

Then she and Annie move back into the crowd. I try to watch them over the heads of the other kids but I'm too short and decide to leave the safety of the wall.

"Annie!"

I'm screaming as loud as I can. "ANNIE!" She turns and runs back to me.

"What's wrong? Did somebody hurt you?" She scans the group, looking for a Pepper to smash. "Did one of the fucking Frogs…"

Ruth is pulling both of us back towards the wall. "They're moving out, come on!" yells Ruth.

She knows the cops will be here soon and wants us to miss the final licks and kicks. We hover by the wall and watch as the sirens pull up. The war is over. Next time it'll be our turn to visit their schoolyard. The only time we get to see the inside of a Pepper school is during the summer. Every year they offer a free breakfast to any kid who attends their summer school programs. The teachers pretend not to notice the large group of English kids trying to fake their way through the cafeteria line-up with their "Bon-jours!" while collecting a plate of eggs and some toast.

I'm not sure if the substitute teachers at Lorne School are rejects from the rich schools too, but they always ask dumb questions right in front of everybody.

"Where is your white shirt, Miss Dobson?"

Some kids have white shirts to wear with their school uniforms but it's not like everybody does. Lots of kids wear T-shirts instead. Me and my sisters don't have white shirts to wear under our uniforms. Mom says they're just a pain in the ass to wash, anyway, and that the clothing room at St. Columba House only gets them once in a blue moon. I've never seen a blue moon in my whole life so just because some kids are lucky enough to see the moon when it's blue and rush down to the clothing room right away and grab a shirt doesn't make them better one bit.

I hope if I don't look at the substitute she'll leave me alone. "I'm sorry, I don't have a white shirt, Miss."

"Excuse me? And who told you I'm a 'Miss'?"

This one is new to Lorne School. She thinks she's going to play with me.

"Hey fuck head," says Spencer. "Why don't you shove your shirt up your ass?"

The teacher looks like she doesn't hear him at first. My face hurts from trying not to grin. Maybe if I pretend I didn't hear what he said, Spencer won't get the strap again. But he pushes his luck. Spencer always does.

"You don't like 'Miss'? How 'bout Mrs. Muff Diving Cunt instead?"

Mom takes me to St. Columba House after school. The moon isn't blue but she says we could always get lucky. I like it when Mom comes with me. When she's with me the ladies let me take as long as I want to when I'm looking at the T-shirts. I'm trying to pick between two that look like they could fit. Do I want the yellow one with the orange and black border? Or the blue one with the large yellow happy face in the middle? I'm pretty sure I want the happy face but it smells funny. Like cat piss on the shower curtain.

"I can wash that at home," says Mom. "But let's see if we can find a white one."

There aren't any white ones except for one that I already know is way too big.

"It won't fit me," I say to my mom. But she's already folding it in half and hanging it off her arm.

"Do you have any socks? Or any underwear in a size 6x or 7?" she asks the two women.

I look back at the funny smelling happy face. Maybe it would fit one of my sisters?

"Mom, I bet that would fit Annie!"

But she still doesn't hear me. She's holding up socks and underwear and smiling at the ladies. I know she's hoping they'll let us take all three. The white T-shirt, socks and underwear.

"Go ahead," says one of the ladies. She smiles at me. I smile back. The moon might not be blue but Mom's found me socks and underwear that will both fit.

When we get home, I give Annie the white T-shirt and she hugs me. I show her my new socks and underwear and she admires the tiny rose on the panties. I didn't see it before. I love them.

I think my dad's looking for a job. Mom says he hasn't had a real job since he stopped being a policeman. He had to quit after Uncle Patrick borrowed his gun. Dad says it was the scariest time in his life. He kept hoping the other policemen wouldn't notice that he didn't have his gun. Dad had to finally go and get the gun back himself from the guys Uncle Patrick loaned it to. They didn't want to give it back, either. Dad says it's because it was so clean they wanted to keep it for a while longer. I don't remember when Dad was a policeman but I've seen the pictures. He looks so handsome. Mom says they made him a policeman just because he was so damn good looking.

"He faked his way through the interview. He faked his way through the job."

Dad says he learned how to write the reports by looking at old files and studying how other officers did it. He taught himself how to spell stuff and how to say what he needed to say, and what was important and what wasn't. Dad says no one ever figured out he quit school when he was in grade four. His handwriting is so neat, too. He gave me the book he used when he was taking a special course on fingerprinting. I didn't even know you had to take a course for that. I think Dad misses being a police officer. One time I said, "Some pigs are here!" when I saw two of them sneaking up on our neighbours next door and Dad got so mad at me.

"Don't you ever call them that! They're police officers and don't you forget it."

I wanted to tell him I was just joking, trying to sound cool. I know police officers are very important and carry guns and shoot bad people and save good people. I mean, not all police officers are good of course. Uncle Luther was a policeman for a while, too, and I know he's pretty mean. He likes to hurt people. Especially kids. One time when he was a kid he tried to set his own little sister on fire after he tied her up, but Dad stopped him.

"Uncle Luther can be a little weird sometimes," says Dad. "Prison is what really ruined him, though. After what they did to him in there, that's where he learned to hurt little boys."

I want to tell Dad that Uncle Luther was hurting little boys, and little girls too, way before he ever went to prison. Grown ups always like him though. After he was caught robbing that bank downtown dressed up to look like a priest, even the judge gave him a break, giving him just a one day sentence after a pastor from the Point promised to work with him on his soul. The *Gazette* ran an article saying the bank teller knew he wasn't really a priest. "He was too good looking," she said.

Holding up a bank wasn't the first time Uncle Luther ever dressed up like a priest. After my baby brother died, Dad sat in the hospital's chapel holding his seven-month-old body, gently rubbing the top of his small head.

"He was just so perfect looking," Dad sometimes tells us after a couple of drinks at the Legion. "His hair showed just a hint of redness and his eyes were so blue."

Dad had just kissed one of his chubby baby cheeks when he saw Uncle Luther standing there, fully dressed for the part.

"Hello Lord!" said Uncle Luther as he looked up at the chapel ceiling. "Yes, I'm speaking to you Lord. I'm speaking to you directly. Look here Lord, look at what I'm showing you, Lord!" and Uncle Luther reached down and placed one of his hands on baby Russell's little head. "Wake him up, Lord. Wake this innocent and raise him up NOW. Do you hear me LORD?"

Dad says a few of the nurses had crowded around the doorway to the chapel and were watching Uncle Luther. My favourite part of the story is when Dad smacks Uncle Luther's hand off baby Russell.

"Don't you touch him!" hissed Dad and Uncle Luther stepped back like Dad had stabbed him in the heart.

Dad wrapped baby Russell back up in the blanket, carefully tucking it in around his tiny hands and toes but leaving his face uncovered. Then he handed his body to one of the nurses and left.

After Uncle Luther did a whole bunch of bank robberies they started calling him the 'Polite Bank Robber' because he always said please and thank you and would give the teller one of his best smiles. Women always like him. He was finally caught by a police helicopter after robbing another bank downtown on St. Catherine Street, and Mom says he'll be going away for a long time.

"You can never tell with some people," says Dad, shaking his head.

I guess he only remembers what Uncle Luther did to that girl in Korea when he's drinking. Dad's hardly ever around, anyway, so I only get to see him when he goes over to Uncle Patrick's. Sometimes I hear them talking about my mom and her new friends.

"Russell, I hear what you're saying, bro," says Uncle Patrick. "I wouldn't allow my wife to hang around with those shit-disturbing commies either. But you have to admit, there's never been a more committed mother…"

Dad interrupts Uncle Patrick.

"But how do I get her away from them, Pat? She's so impressed with their BS it isn't even funny. She's convinced they think she's smart and buys into all of their crap. She doesn't see how they're just using her. She keeps saying she's fighting for 'social justice' whatever the hell that means!"

I feel sorry for Aunt Olive. She always tries to be part of the grown up conversation.

"Some people just aren't the best housekeepers in the world, are they," she says.

When Dad and Uncle Patrick stop talking and stare at her she thinks they're listening.

"Eileen might be a good mother and a real looker and all of that other nonsense but she sure ain't known for her cleaning or cooking."

Aunt Olive smiles and then leans over to take one of Uncle Patrick's cigarettes off the kitchen table. Uncle Patrick smacks her hand away.

"And some people aren't good housekeepers, good cooks, or mothers. And are ugly as sin to boot," says Uncle Patrick.

I really feel bad for Aunt Olive. Uncle Patrick doesn't know he's always hurting her feelings. One time, he asked her if she ever brushes her teeth. Aunt Olive's face got all red and she said yes, she brushes her teeth.

"How close do you stand to the brush?" asked Uncle Patrick.

I want to tell Aunt Olive that she's right though. None of us girls, or my mom, are any good at cooking or cleaning. We wipe our feet off before we get into bed each night or the tiny crumbs will stick to us all night and keep us awake. I hate them. It's like trying to walk with a bunch of tiny rocks in your shoes, except it's even worse because you can't just flip your bed upside down and dump them all out.

Dad has socks to wear when he's in the house so he doesn't have to worry about the crumbs. He just takes his socks off before getting into his bed. But he still has to worry about mice. This one time when he woke up in the middle of the night, he saw a mouse moving around under the blankets. It was a bump near the bottom of the bed. Dad leaned over and grabbed the baseball bat he keeps beside the bed, careful not to move so the mouse wouldn't run away. He raised the bat up high and smashed it down as hard as he could on the lump. Except it wasn't a mouse. It took months for his big toe to heal and even now it doesn't look right.

I want to tell Aunt Olive not to worry. My mom doesn't give a shit what Uncle Patrick thinks of her anyway. I know because she says that all the time. One time I told Mom how Uncle Patrick is the only man, other than Dad, who isn't a creepy pink-eyed pig with me and my sisters. He never looks at us funny or sneaks his hand on our chair just before we sit down or tells us we look hot or tries to touch our buttons.

"Thank god for small miracles," said Mom.

But Aunt Olive is looking down at the floor now and Dad and Uncle Patrick are laughing and talking again.

One time I asked Mom why Uncle Patrick is still mad at Aunt Olive about tricking him and she said it's because she's a Cummings from Gaspé, which means Aunt Olive is even lower on the totem pole than a Richardson. Mom always says it's wrong to treat people differently because of how they look or how much money they don't have. She still asks Aunt Olive sometimes when Uncle Patrick isn't around if she wants to go to one of the Informed Citizen's meetings.

"They have free coffee and babysitting," she says, but Aunt Olive always just shakes her head.

"He'd kill me."

Mom tells her friend Vivian that they have to get more of the other Point mothers to go to their meetings.

"We have to show them just how much power we really have," says Mom to Vivian. "I don't think they realize just how much force we can bring to the table."

Vivian talks just like my mom when they're together. All about force and power and how one voice becomes louder when it's joined by another. Or something like that. Me and my sisters beg Mom to let us go to the next meeting.

"You don't need a babysitter," says Mom, "you're old enough to stay home with Annie and Ruth."

It's not the babysitter we want. It's the oranges and cookies and apple juice the babysitters always give the kids at the meetings. Sometimes they even have stuff left over we can bring home. The oranges are shit, of course, but the cookies and juice are good. Nobody I know in the Point ever eats oranges or any other fruit, except for maybe Jenny but she's rich. Annie says rich people are only pretending to like crap like that. The hippies and commies and lesbians from McGill like shitty food, like yogurt and cheese and oranges, and I guess that's why they bring them to the meetings. They must think we like them too. Mom says the medical students from McGill and nurses are all volunteers who helped set up the first clinic in the Point.

"We aren't alone in this," says Mom. "Not everyone is closing their eyes to the truth down here."

I'm not sure what that all means but I know Mom thinks it's a good thing and she says Dad's wrong to see all these students from McGill as the enemy. She tries to explain it to me.

"Just because someone hasn't ever experienced poverty first hand, or walked the walk, doesn't mean they can't still make an enormous difference. I mean, look at Charlie Larson. He didn't have to get involved. But he's going to change your life, Kathy. He's going to change all of our lives."

I'm afraid to ask her who the hell Charlie Larson is. She might think I wasn't paying attention. Most of the time I really do listen but like Dad sometimes says, once you get Mom going, it's kind of hard to make her stop.

"I gotta go," she says and leaves.

Mom gets two bucks from the social workers to pay a babysitter to watch us at home. She can use the two bucks to buy some bread and Player's Filter and oil for the heater. It means she can't bring us to the meeting, because we're supposed to be at home being watched by a babysitter who's being paid two bucks.

I like it best when they have meetings at our house. The cookies and juice and plastic cups and the untouched oranges all stay after the meeting is over and the people go home. Mom says the student social workers from McGill at the meetings aren't complete assholes yet.

"The system hasn't totally fucked them up yet," she explains.

I like when she explains to them how fucked up they are right to their faces.

"You're being taught to tell us, preach to us, how to fix our problems," Mom says, "instead of asking us, the real experts about our own lives and problems, what we need help with. Don't tell me how to fix my problem—first we need to find a common

56

ground on what exactly my problem is. We need to find a common language."

Belinda Mavory isn't a student social worker. She's already a real social worker. Mom always says she's the only social worker she's ever met who is for real.

"She's not a fake," Mom says to her friends. "She's the real deal."

I like Belinda Mavory too, and so do all my sisters. She's beautiful. She has long hair and white teeth and she looks at you when you talk to her and doesn't try to explain you back to yourself after you tell her stuff. She's the only person I like who isn't from the Point. Dad says her parents are filthy rich, but he says it like that's a bad thing. My dad acts funny around Belinda. He doesn't try to make her laugh and he doesn't tell her she's gorgeous or even that he loves her long hair. I don't know why but I think he's a little afraid of her. But Belinda is one of those people who just make you feel happy whenever she's in the room. I think she really believes everything she says.

"Do you know how lucky you are, Kathy?" she always says to me. "Your mother has nothing, yet look how much she can do. She is one of the most powerful people I have ever met."

My mom loves her too though, which is only fair. I tell Belinda that my mom says it's hard to believe she's a social worker and Belinda laughs. I love it when she laughs. She opens her mouth wide and throws back her head. She makes me feel like she really hears everything I say. Everything. She's a good listener. But I forget how to talk when Belinda suddenly offers to take me for a drive.

"I asked your mom and she said it's okay," says Belinda.

She's smiling at me through her open window. I'm pretty sure she's not a perv but even if she is, she's not that big so I get in. Sometimes Dad has a car but his are usually brand new and huge. The paint on Belinda's car looks like somebody did it with left over house paint. There's stickers of flowers and happy faces on one of the doors.

"What kind of car is this anyway?" I ask so she won't look at my face.

I want her to think it's normal for me to sit in a rich person's car, something I do all the time. I don't know any other women in the Point who drive their own car. Her car is so messy it makes me think of our living room. There's even clothing on the floor and what looks like some food she changed her mind about on the back seat. It has a radio. I'm dying to turn it on.

"It's a Bug," says Belinda. "Sorry for the mess."

But her voice doesn't really sound sorry at all. She sounds happy, like she always does, even if she thinks her car is a bug. I pretend not to notice the pile of stuff near my feet and just gently push it over with my left foot. A hairbrush. Some papers and lots of books. I could stay in Belinda's car forever. When she pulls back in front of our place, I wish I could think of something smart to say.

"Wanna piece of gum?"

I hold out my bag of Yukon Gold. The soft white bag is still nearly full. I've been waiting for something special to happen before I eat most of it.

"Oh, no thanks," says Belinda. "I won't be able to brush my teeth until later and sugar starts to act on your enamel within twenty minutes."

Rich people are so weird. I file it away for later. Maybe Annie can explain what the hell Belinda just said to me.

"Well thanks for the drive," I say.

I'd take the brush if she'd look away for even just a second but she watches me while I jump out of her car. Some kids on the sidewalk across the street are staring at me. I try to look sad. Like my social worker is bringing me back home after a long stay in foster care or something.

"See you later!" says Belinda with a smile and then she pulls away.

I love Belinda's car but I know Dad would think it's a heap of shit. The other day I was coming out of Duffy's Variety when a shiny black Trans-Am pulled up. The windows were all dark so you couldn't see inside. Everyone hanging around the front of the store watched as the car came to a slow stop. People walking by stopped moving and stared at the huge black car with a golden bird painted on the hood. It looked like it should be on a racetrack instead of parked in front of Mr. Duffy's store. Hardly anyone I know in the Point owns a car, never mind a shiny new Trans-Am. The window rolled down and I was surprised to see Dad stick his head out.

"Come here," he said to me.

Everyone standing in front of the store quickly switched their stares from the car to me. I knew what they were thinking. Dad was an undercover cop and I was some informant he was meeting. With a fake frown on my face, I hopped into the car and shut the door behind me.

"They all think you're an undercover cop," I said, which made Dad laugh. I looked through the window and saw that everyone was still gawking at the car. At me. I felt famous.

"Here's some money. I need you to buy some smokes and then meet me at Uncle Pat's place, okay?" Dad said, dropping some money into my hand.

When I got out I looked down at the money in my hand and shrugged. I could feel all the eyes still on me. "Well, I guess I can buy a pack of smokes now," I said.

Other than Dad, the only people I know who have cars are doctors and social workers. Then I remember that Belinda is a social worker. A real social worker. I keep forgetting that. Dad says we should remember not to trust her. He's not saying what bad stuff Belinda might do, but I know she's not the one who tried to talk my mom into giving up Hannah, my baby sister. Hannah is always laughing and banging stuff, making lots of noise.

Annie was babysitting Hannah one time when she suddenly realized Hannah wasn't there anymore. She looked around the yard but couldn't find her.

"Hannah?" she called.

She ran to the front of the house and there was Hannah, waddling onto the street. Mrs. Byrne, our neighbour, was standing in her yard and when she saw the truck speeding towards Hannah, she started screaming. I'm not sure whether the truck driver heard Mrs. Byrne or saw Hannah, but even though he hit the brakes he was too close to stop. Annie ran and jumped and knocked Hannah over just as the truck went by. Hannah was crying from being knocked over, and Mrs. Byrne was crying because she thought Hannah had been hit by the truck. Annie's knees looked like somebody had sprinkled tiny rocks on them, like when Dad puts salt and pepper on his fried eggs.

Last week Hannah was at Nanny's and when it was time to go Dad saw she had peeled off some of the wallpaper. He had to pull a piece out of her mouth. Dad tried taping the pieces back on the wall but he couldn't find them all. Hannah must have swallowed a few. Nanny went on and on about how that old wallpaper had been up on the walls before she was even born. I'm glad Mom didn't give Hannah away like Ruth. Nanny is just a crabby old bitch sometimes. I like her best on Sundays, right after church. Nanny is always happy and in a good mood after she gets home from the Evangel Pentecostal Church. She has to take two buses to get there each Sunday since it's downtown but I think that's part of why she feels so good afterwards. It's hard work going to her church. She says it would be easy to go to the Baptist or Anglican Church in the Point, like we sometimes do with Mom after she's watched too much Billy Graham on TV. Nanny says her church's worship style and teachings come from the Early Church.

"You won't ever see any guitars at the Evangel Pentecostal," says Nanny, like finding a guitar in one of her church's pews would be like stepping on a pile of still warm dog shit.

"We teach the full gospel," says Nanny, "and know His Word is infallible. None of this 'Good news for Modern Man' nonsense either."

Nanny says it's only at her church that a person can receive salvation and all of the Lord's gifts, like speaking in tongues and prophecy. I already told Annie if I ever start chanting like our sister Ruth or one of those other scary people to please slap me before I end up surrounded by a bunch of church members, all eager to place one hand on me and the other stretched out to God, turning me into some kind of fucking zombie lightning rod.

"Man is separated from God," says Nanny, explaining it's because of all the sinning everybody is always doing. But thanks to Jesus not turning all those dirty Jews into stone, Nanny explains, or melting them on the spot like cheap candles, we can get back to God by being born again. I'm not sure how we get born again once we're here the first time but Nanny says anybody who accepts God's gift of salvation gets to go to heaven.

"And those who reject it go to hell."

I wonder who would reject it? I sure don't want to go to hell.

"Going to church and worshipping our Lord publicly is how you walk with Him and welcome the presence of the Holy Spirit," says Nanny.

Her preacher talks like that, too. It's either real boring shit, or real scary shit.

"The Spirit dwells within me!" he bellowed last Sunday from the pulpit. "The Spirit dwells in every Christian. It is our Lord's desire to fill all of his believers with the Holy Spirit after they've asked for and received their salvation."

Then he got to the scary shit.

"When the Dark One tests you, when he comes a knocking, will you be strong enough to hold the door closed to Him? To stand like a rock in the desert, immovable to his demands? His offers of riches and earthly pleasures? WILL YOU?"

That last bit always makes me jump. Asshole. At the Baptist Church in the Point the preacher isn't scary at all. Sometimes he doesn't make sense, but he's never scary.

"What's this?" he says, holding up a broken screen. We all know not to shout out the answer.

"It used to be a screen," says the preacher. "It would sit in a window frame and do a fine job of keeping the bugs out and letting the fresh air in."

He has a way of making the simplest shit sound almost interesting. Even Jamie Moore is sitting there all quiet, staring at the preacher, waiting for him to get to the good part. We all know a good part is coming.

"But now that the screen is broken, the frame is twisted and the screen itself all ripped, what are we to do? Toss it into the garbage? Throw it out to the curb?"

We all jump when the preacher suddenly throws it on the floor.

"It's no longer useful, is it? It no longer has a function or value to us. Or does it?"

Now we're all looking at that torn screen lying in a heap on the floor, wondering what's going to happen to it. I'm even feeling a little sorry for it. What the hell are we going to do next?

"Perhaps that screen could be repaired?" says the Preacher. "Or perhaps it could serve a different function? It seems wasteful, just downright wrong, doesn't it? To simply give up on it?"

Then he bends over and picks it back up again. We all stare at it, wishing it can be fixed somehow. Or turned into something else? Something useful.

"Why can't we care as much when one of our brothers or sisters seem to lose their way in life? Seem to have lost their usefulness to society? Should we toss our fellow man to the curb because in our eyes he no longer has a function? Is too broken to keep?"

Then the guitars come out and we're all singing and smiling and hoping we'll think of somebody we actually know who is broken so we can try and help fix them up.

I like how nobody talks in tongues at the Point church.

"Speaking in tongues is a gift from God," says Nanny. "It's a sign that the believer is being filled with the Holy Spirit. Speaking in tongues means they have a message, like a prophet, for the congregation."

Apparently you need someone with the gift of interpretation to explain what the hell the babbling shit coming out of their mouth actually means. Nanny says listening to someone speaking in tongues is like hearing the language of angels. Me and Annie agree that's just another reason why angels are pretty fucking creepy. Mom hates it when we go to Nanny's church. She says they just preach nastiness.

"I don't know why your grandmother even goes there," says Mom. "They probably just see her as white trash anyway."

We always sit in the same pew, one row up from the black people. One time Nanny asked the usher if we could sit somewhere else, somewhere closer to the front, and he frowned and then brought us one row closer. The next Sunday Nanny went back to her usual pew.

"Coloured folks sure love their pastel colours," said Nanny with a sniff after looking at the row behind us.

Mom says it's a fucking crime how much money Nanny gives to her church.

"It's money she sure as hell can't afford to give away," says Mom, "but if she has to give it, I wish she'd at least give it to one of our churches down here where it could actually do some real good."

Nanny's church is good at asking for money. But sometimes it takes me a few minutes to realize that's what they're even asking for. Annie says the pastors at fancy churches all talk like that. In parables. Just like Jesus.

"Dig deep, my brothers and sisters. Your Lord is asking you to visit the well of generosity again. Our Father knows the depth of your kindness and will smile warmly on you today, knowing you held out your hand when asked to share your bounty with others."

I didn't know that meant he was asking for money until I saw Nanny digging frantically in her purse, trying to find another dollar to give with the one she had put aside for today's offering. When the gold plate passed by for the second time that morning, Nanny dropped another dollar on top of the huge pile of money already filling the plate. I wanted to tell her she didn't have to. That they didn't need her last dollar. I knew she would have just hissed at me that the Lord's Work is more important than buying all of us our popsicles on our way home after church. I always feel ripped off whenever that happens. Without the cherry popsicle afterwards, going to church with Nanny is such a rip off. Sometimes we still get a treat once we get back to her place, but nothing as good as a cherry popsicle. If I help put her in an especially great mood, though, sometimes she brings out the special box of cookies. The Whippets.

"I always love going to your church, Nanny," I say, trying not to grin at my sisters. "At Mom's church they just don't seem to take God and His Word as seriously somehow, you know?"

Nanny puts the kettle on the stove and pulls out the box of Red Rose and the Whippets.

"Yes, but I'm not surprised," says Nanny. "Your mother comes from the Richardsons. You have to remember that. They're not God-fearing Christian people. Your mother and her sisters all lined up at their own father's funeral to spit in his face. Scandalous that was!"

Nanny fans herself with the Red Rose box. I've heard the story about Mom and her spitting sisters about a hundred times and never get tired of the story.

"I know that Mr. Richardson wasn't a decent man," Nanny always adds, "and what he did to those poor girls was a terrible, terrible sin. But retribution and revenge is mine, saith the Lord."

I can sometimes get three cookies out of that story.

"What exactly did he do to those poor sisters of Mom?" I ask, reaching for another cookie.

"Don't even ask me," Nanny says, adding an extra spoon of sugar to my tea. "Don't even ask."

I already knew my mom's father was an icky creep even before Nanny ever said a word about him. No amount of cookies would have me telling her what he liked to do sometimes when alone with any of us girls. Mom must have thought he was harmless by the time us kids were old enough to go over for lunch sometimes because she wasn't afraid to leave us alone with her parents. He did kind of look dead, I admit, sitting there on a stiff chair and not saying a word. I'd hate it when grandma would tell us to say hello and give him a kiss, like the old fucker was deaf or something. None of us wanted to get within kissing range of the creepy prick with his sneaky lizard tongue. I'm glad Mom and her sisters all spit on his dead body. They should have buried him with his tongue and his dick hanging out so the worms could have got to his worst parts first.

Not all of my mom's brothers are pigs. Uncle Ben is Mom's favourite and us girls all like him a lot, too. But if I could have kicked Uncle Eddy into the coffin as they lowered it into the ground, it sure would have saved us kids a whole lot of trouble. My favourite brother of Mom's is Uncle Oscar. One Easter he gave each of us girls a pink basket, filled with tiny chocolate eggs, and a whole bunch of pennies on the bottom.

"Pile all of your pennies right here," said Annie, then after making six equal piles out of the huge mountain in front of her on the floor, we each ended up with almost a hundred pennies.

I like most of my mom's sisters but especially Aunt Alice and Aunt Claire. Aunt Alice is the funniest and loudest person I know and she always brings us a huge bag of cookies when she comes over. Aunt Claire is more quiet but I could look at her forever. She's beautiful, with long red hair, and always smiling. We play a lot with her kids. They live almost next door to Uncle Patrick on Liverpool Street and half the Point hangs out at their place all summer long because of the huge pool her husband sets up in the back each summer. We don't get to see Aunt Alice as much though because she doesn't live in the Point. We like her kids though. They never act snobby about not living in the Point and when we go to visit them they show us how to sneak onto the property near their place that has this swing thing with two benches facing each other and you can move it with your feet. We love to stand on it and make it go as fast as it can until some of the crabby priests who own the place show up and fire their salt and pepper guns at us. Assholes. We call them old fuckers as we run off, laughing so hard we can barely get away. One time our cousin Jasper was hit and got a rash from the top of his shoulder right down the side of his back, but he made us swear not to tell anyone what happened. I think it's because he knew that if Aunt Alice found out, she'd go back and shove the salt and pepper gun right up that old priest's ass. Aunt Alice's house is even messier than ours, with clothes all piled up in huge heaps all over the place. I always feel warm and happy there, laughing with our cousins and eating the ton of food Aunt Alice always shares with us. I feel embarrassed when they come to our place and we have to pretend we were just about to go and get some groceries. They never act mean about it though.

"We all just ate," says Aunt Alice in that loud friendly voice of hers. "So we just brought dessert!" and then she plops that bag of cookies down.

I wish we could see them more often but Mom says Aunt Alice's life is "complicated."

"Alice does the best she can with what she has," says Mom.

Me and my sisters always love going to the street parties that my mom and her friends set up. Traffic is blocked off and a big truck drives in, taking up the whole street, and when the side of the truck lifts up there's a band sitting inside. But nobody comes for the music. Everybody comes for the free hotdogs and cokes. There's also lots of other good stuff like chips and Cheezies. There's also always a bunch of weird shit on the picnic tables that nobody touches—soggy fruit all chopped up in a huge bowl, tiny sandwiches with stinky crap in them, and some other stuff I don't even recognize. But at least with the street parties there aren't any oranges taking up table space. Nearly everybody stays away from the hot dogs though after we hear they were donated by Joe's at the corner. Ever since one of his fingers went missing, everybody's too grossed out and nervous to eat his hotdogs. When I spot Annie eating one, I can't help myself.

"You know Joe's finger is in there, right?"

The feminist agitators move through the crowd and talk to people, trying to pretend they're having fun while handing out balloons. Most people politely listen while they eat their hotdogs and avoid the weird shit. After a while the band stops playing and the feminists give some speeches.

"You are not alone. You are not one voice!"

Somebody yells, "Suck me off baby!" and a few people laugh.

When the street party is over, I ask Annie what a "feminist agitator" is and she says it's for cleaning the inside parts of your muff.

Anita and Judy and Vivian and all the other Point mothers agree with my mom, nodding their heads while she explains why the student social workers at McGill have to be careful. The meeting is at our kitchen table. With all the bodies crowded around, there's barely enough room for all the ashtrays, coffee mugs, and muffins that one of the rich people have brought. They nod and smile when my mom explains how crucially important it is for student social workers not to become complete assholes by the time they aren't students anymore, and how all the mothers in the kitchen just want to save the students from being fucked over by McGill.

"We have to reach them before it's too late," says Mom, "while they're still open to learning and don't think they already have all the answers."

Dad laughs when he hears that Mom's been invited to speak at McGill in front of the student social workers.

"How in the hell did you manage to pull that off?" laughs Dad.

Mom sounds proud as she brags to Dad about what others are saying about the Point groups she's involved with.

"We're known for being among some of the most confrontational and autonomous in the province," says Mom.

When she shows him the cheque they gave her at McGill just for telling the school of social work what total fuck ups they're all going to be one day, he says he's in the wrong line of work.

"You don't have any line of work," says Mom. Dad slams the door as he leaves.

Mom worked hard for that cheque. She wrote and wrote for days before she took the bus to McGill.

"Don't let the system tell you who we are and what we need," my mom says to the crowded room of students. "Let us, let me, a real live breathing poor person tell you what we need. I'm here. Right here right now. Please. Reach out and touch me."

Dad laughed after he read Mom's speech for McGill out loud. "I can't believe they paid you to beat up on them. What's wrong with these people?"

At the kitchen table, Mom starts to get wound up. She's

67

explaining how just because somebody wants to change the world, it doesn't mean they get to change it to fit what they think the world should look like. I hate it when my mom talks like that. It just means that when everybody leaves she'll be loud for hours and hours, trying to get out all the words she forgot to say when everybody was still here.

"What the hell will they do when we finally rise up and instead of saying 'please' and 'thank you,' crossing our t's and dotting our i's and watching our p's and q's, we just TAKE what is ours? Eh? What will the assholes do then?"

Mom doesn't want me to answer. Just listen. Until I forget to listen and then jump when she gets loud again.

"When will people wake up and see how fucking used and abused we all are? We deserve our share! Our FUCKING SHARE!"

Then Mom writes it all down and says it's gold for the next sit-in and ass kicking at the welfare office or school board. She makes me nervous when she shouts, "I AM NOT AFRAID!"

Dad says Mom was an actress in another life. Annie thinks we're going to get to stay home from school again tomorrow. Mom says she's planning to teach the school board something about people without power.

"Labels aren't always dangerous or limiting," says Mom as she writes it all down. "How can you own what you can't name?"

I hope it doesn't rain. I hate lying on the street when it's wet.

Chapter Four

I DON'T REMEMBER THE EXACT DAY I figured out that my sister Ruth is a vampire but I do remember why I stopped trying to warn everybody. It just gets me into trouble.

"Stop talking like that! You sound like an idiot," Mom said. "You and I both know your sister is not a damn vampire."

But my mom is wrong. Not that Ruth has ever tried to bite me or suck my blood or anything. Everybody knows that vampires don't mess with their own families. At least, I'm pretty sure they don't. But no matter how many times I've tried explaining about all the proof, like Ruth's fangs and what she does to flies, no one believes me.

"Those aren't fangs," Annie laughed. "They're just bread!"

Maybe fangs made of bread don't seem as evil as fangs made of, well, whatever the other kind of fangs are made of. But fangs are fangs, right? I figure that's just Annie's way of trying to be supportive. Annie is always on your side if you're a sister. I mean, I won't tell anyone but another sister if I ever find one of Ruth's dead bodies, the blood all sucked out of it. I'm just like Annie when it comes to supporting sisters, no matter what. But that doesn't mean Ruth isn't still kind of scary and I just want everyone to know about her. I'm thinking she might bring other vampires to our house, ones that maybe won't respect the never-bite-a-sister rule.

Annie tried to make me feel okay by explaining why Ruth can't be a vampire.

"If Ruth is a vampire, someone must have bit her, right? Do you know anyone else in the Point who could be a vampire?"

Annie is so smart. I'd never even thought of that. Nanny took Ruth away from Mom when she was a baby and even though Ruth started living with us again later, she spends a lot of time at Nanny's house. But Nanny can't be a vampire. If she looked in the mirror and saw Satan's fangs sticking out of her mouth, she'd probably put a stake in her own heart.

Annie made me feel better for a little while, but then I realized that whoever bit Ruth could live far away from the Point and I wouldn't even know them.

"I know you're a vampire," I say to Ruth one day, when we're alone in the kitchen.

She smiles at me. Then shows me her teeth.

"You wouldn't bite me, right? I'm your sister. Vampires don't mess with their own flesh and blood... right?"

Ruth gives me one of her mean smiles. "I thought you said I'm not your sister?"

Shit. She's right. I did say that. Sort of.

"No, I said you aren't the 'oldest.' I never said you aren't my sister."

Whew. She looks like she's thinking it over. Ruth wants to be the boss of all of us girls, but it's too late. She's always been Nanny's girl.

"But I AM the oldest," Ruth says. "I was born first, before you were. I knew you before you knew you. I saw you when you still couldn't open your baby eyes. I saw your diaper poops and pees and Mom giving you a bottle and everything."

Ruth is just lining up the proof that she's one of us since she was there at the beginning. I figure it's okay to let a vampire win that fight.

"You never saw any of my poops," I tell her. I need a second to think. I don't want to argue about whether it's okay or not for her to bite me. To drink my blood. Baby shit is a whole lot safer to talk about.

"I did so!" Ruth argues. "I even helped Mom change your diapers sometimes."

I ignore the lie.

"You can't hurt somebody you used to know as a baby, right?" I'm still feeling hopeful.

Then Annie comes in the room and asks what we're doing. Ruth laughs and says she should ask me.

"I'm asking Ruth to please never bite me or suck my blood or do any vampire stuff with me when I'm sleeping," I say to Annie.

I'm so tired of sleeping with my blanket rolled up and wrapped around my neck like a donut. My head hurts when I wake up every morning. I wish I had some garlic or a cross or some Holy water. Well, maybe not Holy water. I can't do anything mean or gross like throw it in Ruth's face and watch her cheeks melt away like they're on fire. But a cross or a Bible that will make her back off if I ever catch her sneaking up on me would be good. Maybe Aunt Mary or Nanny will lend me their Bible for a while. Especially if I pretend I want to read it. To help me finally nail the Ten Commandments for Sunday school at Nanny's church.

"You gotta stop messing with her," Annie says. Her and Ruth laugh. "Seriously, she's scared shitless and afraid to fall asleep now."

I wish I could punch Annie right in the face. Telling Ruth I'm afraid of her? Annie knows you can't let anybody know when you're afraid of them. Shit.

"I'm not scared shitless," I say, then give both of them my meanest look.

Ruth never takes the blood from flies. Just their wings. The first time I saw her pull the wings off a fly I thought she was trying to stick them back on. I knew she didn't have any glue or tape and figured maybe she was licking the wings to make them stick on the flies.

"What are you doing?" I asked, then sat down on the floor next to her. For a second she hunched over the bowl on the floor in front of her, then she sat up straight.

"They need to learn how to walk. Flying is easy when you have wings."

Then she opened her hand and showed me inside. Ruth was holding another fly. She reached down and carefully ripped its wings off, then dropped the wings onto a small pile on the floor next to her. Then she put the fly into the large plastic bowl with the other flies and watched for a moment as it started running frantically around the bottom of the bowl. I was surprised there wasn't any blood, even though there must have been a dozen wingless flies crawling around in the bowl. The pile of wings didn't have any blood on them either.

"What are you going to do with all those wings?" I didn't want to bring up the missing blood.

Mom always says that flies carry the worst filth, even worse than cockroaches. At least cockroaches know to run away as soon as you make any movement. Flies will barf and shit on your food, then come right back the moment you act all still and stuff.

"It's a secret," said Ruth.

I decided not to tell her that no matter how many wings she tried to pile up, they'd never be able to help her fly. They're just too small. I held my breath, afraid to breathe, when Ruth suddenly leaned over and started crushing all the wingless flies. Ruth can just be so mean sometimes. After she walked away I looked down and saw all the wings on the floor still in a small pile next to the bowl. I tried to sweep them up into my hands but they fell apart like dust.

When Ruth says she has a secret, it always turns out to be boring and something that anybody with half a brain could guess. Last week she told Annie and me that Aunt Mary is crazy. Like we didn't already know that.

"No seriously, she was in a nut house! One of those houses for crazy people that have papers from doctors and everything saying they're officially crazy. Nuts. With a whole bunch of other crazy people, too."

Like I said. Boring. I looked at her and yawned, just to make Annie laugh. Ruth got so mad at me.

"Oh, go ahead and be a Miss Smarty Know it All. But Aunt Mary's one of those crazy people who hears voices in her head."

Okay, that was a tiny bit interesting. I was willing to play.

"What are the voices saying to her?"

"Wouldn't you like to know!" said Ruth.

See what I mean? Major pain in the ass.

"I knew you were just making that up," Annie said, and then winked at me.

"I am NOT," said Ruth. "Nanny told Uncle Lawrence that's why she's letting Aunt Mary move in with her. The landlord at Aunt Mary's place is kicking her out. She's creeping out all her neighbours, saying they're trying to live in her head for free and telling her to do stuff."

"Stuff?" Now I had to know. "Stuff like what?"

"What do you think?" said Ruth. I always hate it when she uses that bossy voice, the one that says I'm stupid and she's smart. "They're telling her to do very bad things."

Aunt Mary would never hurt anybody. She's too old and weak and can't move very fast and can't even talk to people. And she isn't mean at all, even though she creeps out my cousin Dennis and even some of my sisters. She just says weird stuff sometimes. Like when she told us that she uses Listerine all the time to kill the sin in her mouth, "Because the mouth is a major portal for imps and all kinds of evil."

I don't think Nanny knows how mean she can sound sometimes, like when she told Aunt Mary that she lives to eat, but Nanny eats to live. And that Aunt Mary is built just like a spider.

"A big round gut in the middle with skinny legs."

Aunt Mary laughed but I could tell it hurt her feelings. When Nanny went to the bathroom I told Aunt Mary that Nanny was wrong, she doesn't look like a spider. She smiled at me and said, "Hush. She'll hear you."

Dennis started living with Nanny around that time. After she had to give Ruth back, she stole Dennis from Aunt Olive and Uncle Patrick, saying she didn't want him to get any beatings that would make him simple in the head and grow up like his older brother Marvin, who's afraid of everybody all the time and colours in all the o's in the newspaper.

Dennis is so afraid of Aunt Mary. One time Annie and me dared him to do a combat crawl into her bedroom at Nanny's and stick a plastic rat on the end of her bed. Except for meal times Aunt Mary is nearly always in bed. I'm not sure what Dennis was afraid she'd do if she caught him, but me and Annie know Aunt Mary would never hurt him. Or anybody.

"If you do it," Annie said, "I'll do your homework for a week."

Dennis doesn't give a shit if anyone does his homework or not. Especially himself.

"If you don't," I said, "you're just pure chickenshit."

Dennis started crawling. We watched from the hallway, hidden in shadows, trying not to bust a gut and start laughing. Nanny would get mad if we woke up Aunt Mary.

"I don't need some bored paranoid nut hanging around and pestering me in the kitchen when I'm trying to do my work. Just leave her be in dream land where she belongs, thank you very much."

Dennis dragged his body along the floor inch-by-inch, getting closer and closer to Aunt Mary's bed. He kept looking back at us with a scared face, like he was worried we might do something nasty like shut the door on him all the way. As if we could ever be that mean. Every time he looked back at us, we'd wave our hands at him, trying to push him forward and closer to her bed with our faces. He had just reached the side of her bed when it happened. He lifted the rat towards the bed and looked back at us triumphantly. And then he saw the look on our faces. Even before her hand reached down and made contact, he was screaming. She grabbed him by the top of his hair and started yelling.

"You damn little imp. He sent you here, didn't He? I command you to LEAVE. I COMMAND YOU!"

Annie and I coco butted each other as we turned and tried to run down the hallway at the same time. I almost knocked Nanny over when she rushed towards Dennis's terrified screams. I was laughing so hard I couldn't yell to Annie to hurry up. We caught up with each other outside on the sidewalk. We knew we wouldn't be able to go back to Nanny's for a while.

Later, while Dennis pounded my arm, I kept trying to tell him I knew Aunt Mary would never hurt him. She was just sick from never letting all the tears come out when the bad things happened to her when she was little and wasn't allowed to cry. I told her one time that since she's all grown up, she can cry anytime she wants to now and no one will get mad at her or tell her she's not allowed to. She smiled at me and said I was her special little angel. Annie laughed when I told her Aunt Mary called me her little angel.

"She's going to send you to heaven one day, alright," Annie said. I told Annie she was just jealous because Aunt Mary likes me best.

Of course, Aunt Mary can be embarrassing sometimes. Before she moved in with Nanny I used to go grocery shopping with her sometimes. We'd take the 79 bus on Charlevoix and go downtown to the Steinberg's on St. Catherine's. Sometimes everything would go okay and Aunt Mary would buy a chicken already cooked and when we got back to her place, after all the groceries were put away, she'd give me a whole leg to eat all by myself. Sometimes she'd give me a molasses cookie with a cup of tea, too. But other times, when we were at the check-out in the grocery store and I thought it was safe to relax, she'd suddenly have one of her spells and start asking the girl at the cash register why was she listening to the imps and trying to put a hex on her. One time on the bus she told me in a real loud voice that I shouldn't sit too close to anybody, because everyone had lice and smelt like musty old vaginas. I felt my face go all hot and I just stared at the floor and hoped the driver wouldn't kick us off the bus. It was no use pretending that maybe I didn't even know her, like this old lunatic had just decided to start talking to me. And no matter what I said, I couldn't get her to change her mind or to be quiet. Once she started letting those ugly thoughts out she'd get herself all worked up. I waited until we got back to her place so I could run down to Nanny's and tell her Aunt Mary was acting crazy again. Nanny grabbed her coat and purse and we ran back over together.

In the short time it took me to go and fetch Nanny and come back again, Aunt Mary had covered up every single window in her apartment with newspapers.

"Ruth," Aunt Mary said as soon as she saw Nanny with me,

"He's sending them to me again. They're coming up through the floors and through the walls."

That's about the only time I've ever seen Nanny being nice to Aunt Mary.

"Mary, stop this nonsense. You know you'll have to go back if you don't get a hold of yourself right this minute before you lose complete control again. Just pay no mind to all of that foolishness, you know it's all in your head. Have you been taking your pills?"

And when Aunt Mary nodded, Nanny said, "Show me."

Ever since Aunt Mary moved in with Nanny, she's been quiet most of the time, either reading her Bible or sleeping. She hardly ever says people are trying to steal her thoughts or set themselves up in her head rent-free anymore. But I miss going shopping with her. And I miss that chicken. Those chicken legs were so good.

Ruth says she has another secret but I don't think it's one of her usual boring ones. She keeps telling us we have to take it to the grave and never tell anybody, especially not Mom.

Annie asks Ruth what the secret is. Annie is nice like that. I would have kept pretending not to have heard Ruth. Once you wind Ruth up she's like an old person. She won't stop yakking at you until she runs out of breath or you walk away.

"You have to swear you won't ever tell anybody," Ruth says. Her voice is shaking. She wants us to beg her.

"What?" Annie asks. "What is it?"

"The Devil took me last night."

What? The Devil? He took her?

"What do you mean the Devil took you? Where'd he take you?" Annie asks.

Ruth starts crying. Now I'm really scared.

"He took me… down there…"

He took her to hell?

"Where do you mean?" asks Annie. She sounds mad.

"He made me a woman," says Ruth.

He made her a woman? More like a goat with fucking horns. See how annoying she is? Ruth is too special for Uncles or that perv on Liverpool Street. When she gets fucked with, it's by the Devil. See how messed up she is? I know it's not her fault. If I'd been stolen by Nanny when I was just a baby, I know I'd be acting like one of those kids who grow up all alone with just grown ups, too. Sometimes she just bugs the crap out of me.

It's not just the Devil who has touched her, either. Nanny says Ruth has been touched by God, too. That's why she has the tongues. I hope God doesn't know what's in my heart like Nanny always says because if he does, he knows I just want to slap Ruth when she starts yakking and being all loud and speaking like someone from a different country. I'm sure she's faking. And maybe even thinks we're all stupid for believing her.

I once asked Ruth, "If God is so powerful and all-knowing and all-seeing and all that, how come he can't understand plain English? Why do people have to talk to him like they've gone retarded?"

"You're just jealous," Ruth said in her bossiest voice, "of my close relationship with the Lord. That I walk and talk with Him and you don't."

Walk and talk with him? Holy shit. Does he know she's a vampire? What does He think of how she treats his creatures, ripping their wings off and crushing them? Nanny says all living things are God's creatures. Even flies. I wonder what God thinks about her being made a woman by you know who.

"Did you tell the Lord?" I ask Ruth. She tells me to fuck off.

Annie asks if it hurt.

"Of course it hurt!" says Ruth. "Nanny is going to pray for me. She says once the Devil gets a taste of what he really likes, he always comes back for more."

He always comes back for more? Shit, I wish Ruth would stay at Nanny's full-time again. I don't want the Devil to maybe make a mistake and visit the wrong bunk bed set when he comes back for another visit.

Mom has started putting Ruth in charge sometimes when she goes off to her meetings. I hate it when Ruth babysits us. Annie plays with us and reads us stories. Ruth talks about how messy everything is and how we're eating too much, even though she knows there's no food in the house, and that we should surprise Mom by cleaning up and putting stuff away. Then she makes us go to bed, even when we tell her that we won't make a sound when Mom comes home.

"It's a school night," Ruth says. "You have to get your sleep."

Annie pretends that she thinks Ruth is in charge and lets her boss us around.

"Want me to read them a story, Ruth?" she asks.

I'm hoping Ruth will go back to Nanny's soon but I don't think she will. Even though Nanny just bought her a budgie and every-thing.

"How'd you get Nanny to buy you a bird?" I ask her. I couldn't help it.

"I told her I wanted a pet," says Ruth. "I wanted a cat but Nanny says they eat too much and a budgie is better than nothing."

"Yeah, but it's a French bird," I say. "It keeps saying 'Bonjour! Bonjour!'"

"No, it's a bilingual bird," says Ruth. "Nanny's teaching it stuff to say, and so is Dad."

She's right. The bird does speak both English and French. It freaks me out a little though when I'll be sitting at the kitchen table having a cup of tea and the stupid bird will suddenly squawk, "Praise the Lord! Praise the Lord! Bonjour! Pass the ammunition, squaaawk!"

Ruth decided to call the bird "Sugar." She told Nanny it's because it's so sweet. Nanny always believes that shit when Ruth says it. But I know that poor Sugar is just going to be the first meal for Ruth's cat one day. If she's saying she wants a cat, it's only a matter of time.

"If you said you want a cat, you know Nanny is going to get you one," I say.

"No she won't," says Ruth. "I'm not her favourite anymore. Now Dennis is. Now Dennis will get everything he wants. Nanny has a boy now."

Annie says Ruth's got the only Christian bird in the Point and I can tell Ruth's not sure if Annie's just messing with her or not.

"Nanny's going to get all the French out of it," says Ruth. "She sticks it under the tap now every time it says Bonjour."

When Mom gets back from her meetings, sometimes she doesn't mind if we're still awake. Then we get to ask her all about the meeting. How many people were there? Did anyone fight? Did the police come?

Mom was at a protest on Congregation Street, marching up and down half a city block of cold water flats, when the landlord's son showed up and started snapping pictures of the demonstrators. "That prick wants to blackball them," explains Mom. "Someone should have smashed his camera, the fucker. These landlords never fix a thing in their goddamn firetraps and then expect us to take it lying down."

Mom says how in one family's place the pipes burst and the family had to live with a skating rink right inside their apartment and no water for more than two weeks because the landlord wasn't heating the ground floor apartment.

"That landlord owns 1,200 housing units in the Point and he never sets foot in any of them."

There was even an article about it in the *Gazette* that said there were icicles hanging from the ceiling. After that, instead of demonstrating in front of the cold water flats, Mom and the other protestors went and demonstrated in front of the landlord's home in Montréal West. He finally agreed to heat the building like he was supposed to.

Mom says we won't always be at the mercy of slum landlords.

"You girls are all going to attend a real school one of these days," Mom tells us. "With decent books and first class teachers, you'll get a legitimate education. My girls are all going to be high school graduates!"

Mom is fighting to make one of the rich kid schools in Westmount take us as students. She says we're going to be guinea pigs one day. I don't want to sound rude or anything, so I don't tell Mom that I don't really want to be a guinea pig when I grow up. Maybe the rich kids in Westmount want to be guinea pigs but I want to be a writer. Mom always says I'm good at making up stories about everything. Annie says she wants to be a vet or a nurse and a welfare mom with six kids.

"And I'll make lists of everything I need to buy and a list for all my bills. I'll plan everything and write down what foods to buy for my kids each week and what meals I should cook."

Annie's smart like that. She's always making lists. Lists of what homework she has to do, lists of what stuff she's going to buy one day if she ever becomes rich. She's going to be ready, no matter what happens.

"What about a husband?" I ask and Annie snorts.

"No, I want to be in charge of me and everything else."

Mom is always writing stuff too, but it isn't lists. She says they're articles about what it's like to be a young mother on welfare, alone with six kids.

"And how the movement has impacted my life and belief system."

I want to ask her about Dad. Mom isn't always alone. Sometimes Dad comes over for fried eggs and to explain to Mom what she's doing wrong. Sometimes he even sleeps over and stays for days and days. But I don't want to make her mad so I don't ask. Sometimes she stays up late writing at the kitchen table. One time she said she likes to write about what makes her angry and what scares her. I was surprised. I didn't think anything scared Mom.

"Everybody has fears," Mom said.

I wonder what Dad's fears are? Dad said everyone needs one person they can always tell the truth to.

"You mean, like their secrets?" I asked.

"No," said Dad. "That's different. Some secrets should never be shared."

I think I know one of Dad's fears, though. Getting shot. A few days ago he went to the Bank of Montréal on Wellington Street with Nanny and after he pulled the door open for her to step through, she almost got knocked over by two young guys rushing out. It bugged the crap out of Dad that they didn't even stop to say they were sorry or anything, so Dad gave one of them a little shove and said, "Hey, you need to learn some manners." That made the guy stop and turn around and he told Dad to go fuck himself. Big mistake. After Dad grabbed him by the neck, they both went tumbling down the bank's steps and Nanny ran inside to get help, sure these two young guys were going to beat the crap out of Dad. At first she didn't understand why everyone in the bank was lying on the floor, face down, with their hands over the back of their heads. Just as Nanny came screeching back out of the bank, yelling, "Russell! They're bank robbers!" the other bank robber suddenly stuck a gun right up against Dad's temple and said, "Cool it."

My dad immediately unwrapped his hands from around the other guy's neck and slowly backed away.

"I'm cool. I'm cool," he said with his hands held out in front of him.

The two bank robbers ran off and when the police showed up they asked Dad for a description.

"I described them wrong on purpose," Dad told us later. Nanny said that was just nonsense.

"Why did you do that? One of them held a gun to your head, Russell. He could have shot you. Killed you!" she said.

"But he didn't shoot me," said Dad. "He didn't kill me."

When Dad saw one of them a couple of days later at the pool hall they just looked at each other and then looked away. Dad was different for a while after that. He started telling Mom she needed to be more careful when she's yelling through one of her bullhorns and the police show up. Mom and her friends taught us all to just fall down, like we're dead when the police try to make us move. Then they have to drag us, and Mom and her friends say they don't like pulling on kids.

"Be smart, Eileen. They won't hesitate to bust your teeth," says Dad. "Some of those loud mouths with you are going to get you all into serious trouble one of these days."

I wonder if Dad ever busted any teeth when he was a policeman. Mom asks Dad if she saw him spying on her at the last protest in front of the school board's offices.

"I wasn't spying," Dad tells her. "I just want to keep an eye on you."

Mom smiles and tells Dad that she's going to make a believer out of him yet.

"We're this close to getting some of our kids into Westmount Park and Westmount High," Mom says, "this close. I think it would make a huge difference if they saw more of the fathers coming to our sit-ins, showing them that these kids actually have two parents that give a shit."

Mom keeps trying to pull Dad back to us. I want to tell her that she's using the wrong stuff but I don't want to make her mad. I wonder why Dad ever comes back at all. Mom doesn't cook, clean, or even know to be really nice to him when he's around. Oh, she'll fry him up some eggs if we have any and sometimes she'll even make him peanut butter cookies and let us each have one, too. But whenever Dad goes away for a while Mom is calmer and reads to us every night again. All six of us crowd together on her bed, watching her face as she acts out the story in her forehead and eyes. When Dad came back one time before she had finished *The Wizard of Oz*, it was the first time I secretly wished he'd hurry up and go away again.

"Why would you want our kids to be part of some circus act, anyway?" Dad asks. "They'll stand out like sore thumbs in those schools. They'll be treated like freaks and lepers."

I'm dying to ask what a leper is. I thought they only had those in the Bible.

"Our kids have the right to a decent education, Russell. Don't you want more for them? Do you want your girls to grow up dependent on some man?"

Dad says he might go to the next meeting and Mom makes him some coffee. When I wake up the next morning, he's still drinking it at the kitchen table, him and Mom smiling at each other.

When he leaves, Mom pulls out her notebook and starts writing. She writes articles for *The Boiling Point* now, a newspaper you can get for free in the Point. Dad calls it a rag.

"It's just a bunch of crap written by some over-educated Reds who know exactly how to get people riled up."

But Mom disagrees and says it's a newspaper for the people, a newspaper that only tells the truth.

"Right," says Dad. "And directions on how to stir the pot just to be a major pain in the butt. That's a real newspaper alright."

I ask Mom what the article she's working on is about. Sometimes Mom reads her stuff out loud to us. Her new friends call her an amazing writer and say that her anger and truth are so fresh on the page, the words practically jump off and bite you. Dad laughed when I asked him how that's even possible, words jumping off a page and biting you.

"Pure bullshit can move mountains," Dad said, "and your mother is the queen and complete master of bullshit."

I know not to tell Dad that I think Mom's friends, the Outsiders, are right about some stuff. Mom does get mad when she writes and sometimes acts like she wants to hit something after she's finished.

"The truth doesn't set me free," she says. "It just pisses me off."

All her new friends take notes.

"There's lots more of where that came from," Mom says with a smile.

Belinda Mavory said that my mom is a powerful writer. Or maybe Belinda said writers are powerful?

"Words won't put food on the table or in a hungry belly," scoffs Nanny when I tell her Mom is writing for the newspaper now.

"That isn't a real newspaper," she says after I show her Mom's words on the page.

"Words don't matter if they don't pay you nothing. Nobody reads that anyhow."

I know it would be rude to tell Nanny that everybody reads the *The Boiling Point*. It's full of information about what's going on in the Point. Mom says it's the only newspaper you can trust.

"It's by the people," she says.

Dad just thinks Mom sounds like a commie.

"Do you know how stupid that sounds coming out of your mouth, Eileen? All your new little friends are just playing at being poor. They think it makes them more real or authentic or something but trust me, as soon as they get tired of eating bologna or Kraft Dinner or potato chips for supper, or get tired of stepping on roaches and watching mice piss all over their counters, all they have to do is walk away."

Are we having bologna or Kraft Dinner? Did Mom buy some chips? I can't wait to tell the girls. My stomach wakes up and I try not to grin. I need to stay invisible. I want to listen.

"When was the last time you fed your kids, Russell? Huh? Can I send them over to your mother's tonight and have her fry them up a couple of eggs? Eh? Maybe some toast to go with it on the side?"

We all know Dad can't stand living in filth. A few days earlier he tried filling a crack in the wall where the roaches lived, but it was hard because he was doubled over and leaning away from the crack, making a retching noise every couple of seconds. The roaches started to fall out of the wall the instant Dad made his first pass at the crack, their backs coated with plaster. Like someone had flicked pudding at them. Dad tried to cover the crack even faster but the roaches fought back by scurrying around and trying to make him puke. They finally won. For the next few weeks we would spot a white-speckled roach every once in a while. One of Dad's roaches.

Dad's always had a weak stomach when it comes to bugs. He told us that when he was fighting the gooks in Korea, his weak stomach had to hide for a little while.

"I was so hungry in the beginning because I couldn't eat anything over there at first. Their local crap had shit in the rice, the fish was raw, and the water was dirty. The army kept warning us not to eat anything but our rations. Ma sent me some stuff later but it would be months before her parcels would catch up with me."

Finally he had no choice. Dad says he was starving to death so he had to start eating the meals they dared to call "food." He says

84

how everything in the army comes in its own little box or pouch or tin, a perfect portion. I think that's how Annie would eat all her food if she could, from perfectly organized and measured containers.

"The only part worth eating was the small pudding cup. I'd always save it for last."

Dad is such a good storyteller. He's told us that story a million times and we all know what happens next, but we still hope it ends differently. That he'll open up the pudding cup and everything will be perfectly fine and he'll get to eat his dessert.

"I peel back the lid and I'm about to dig in when sure enough, doesn't a damn wasp go flying by and land right smack in the middle of my double vanilla pudding cup!"

Dad always makes a bit of a gagging noise at this point and swallows hard a few times, looking like this time he'd really do it-he was really going to hurl. Sometimes I have to take a few hard swallows myself.

"That thing was flapping around, digging itself even deeper in my vanilla pudding and that's when something inside of me just kind of snapped, I guess. I took the tip of my spoon and just flicked the damn bug right out of my cup. Then I ate the rest of the pudding without a thought."

We know not to ask any questions while Dad tells the story. That would be breaking the rules. But I always want to ask what happened to that wasp. Did it crawl away, licking the pudding off itself once it got to safety? You know, like under a rock somewhere? And could it ever fly again? Once it got its wings all cleaned up and stuff? Or did Dad just stomp the wasp, crushing it under his big army boot, punishing it for stealing some of his pudding? After that, Dad never minded eating anything else while he was in Korea. But when he came home after the war, his weak stomach was waiting for him in Montréal. Sometimes when Mom offers to cook him something he'll look around the kitchen and snort in disgust.

"In this filth?" Then he'll leave and stay at Nanny's for a while. Her place is always clean.

Sometimes when me or my sisters wash our hair in the kitchen sink at Nanny's place we'll promise to pay Dennis a nickel to stand behind us and watch the crack in the ceiling over the sink. He's the Roach Spotter, and it's his job to warn us if one of them come crawling out of the crack and is in danger of falling on our heads.

One time, my head was under the water but I could hear a weird banging noise coming from above.

THUMP. THUMP THUMP. THUMP.

I stood up and saw Dennis holding a broom, whacking the ceiling and trying to knock some roaches loose. He couldn't stop laughing. The little shithead was paying me back for Aunt Mary.

"Now you're never gonna get that nickel!" I yelled as I chased him down the hallway.

"You know you were never gonna pay me anyway!" laughed Dennis.

Mom sits at the kitchen table and reads her article again. She says it's important to pick just the right word and get all the sentences in perfect order.

I nod my head and pretend I know what she's talking about even though I know she's not really talking to me. If I'm quiet, she might read the whole thing out loud again. I love listening to Mom read. She can make anything sound interesting. Even her speeches. When she hears the buzzer go for the guy next door, our neighbour Mr. Cox, she notices me standing there.

"Go get Ruth and Annie," she says. "Quickly!"

I know what Mom is planning. We did it one time just before Christmas last year. I'm so excited I have to remind myself to be as quiet as possible. I float down the staircase like a ghost and find Ruth and Annie around the corner playing hopscotch with Danielle. Her hair is wet and she smells like vinegar. Everybody in the Point knows what that means.

"You got bugs?" I ask without thinking and then wish I could take it back.

"Shut up," says Ruth.

"Mr. Cox is getting a delivery from Steinberg's and he's at church." I say it like I've been running for miles, almost out of breath.

They say bye to Danielle and run home with me. When we get to the stairs, the large box is already off the truck and sitting in front of his door. Mom is waiting inside. As soon as the three of us get the box halfway into the landing, Mom leans over and helps us get it up the stairs. We haul it into the kitchen and drop it on the floor in front of the table. At first we just stare at the box. It's like that moment on Christmas morning when you first look at the stuff under the tree and you don't know yet what Santa might have brought. Everything looks great and you're dying to know but you're also secretly a little bit scared that maybe he got it wrong. Maybe when you unwrap your gifts you'll realize it's another Christmas from the Salvation Army and instead of a doll with beautiful long hair, you've got a clown with an ugly hat and a scary face. Maybe Mr. Cox just had all his cat food and cleaning stuff delivered. Mom leans over to unwrap the gift.

"Oh my god," she whispers, then sits down on one of the kitchen chairs.

There's tins of beans, bread, a huge bag of white margarine, a big jar of peanut butter. Ruth leans over to lift some stuff up and we see there's more underneath. Even a box of Rosettes. I look at my sisters and we smile. Mom is crying but I know she'll be okay. It's just the shock and all.

"Not a word, girls," she says. "Not a word."

If we don't say it out loud then it doesn't count. We know the rules. When Mr. Cox knocks on our door that night we just ignore it. People in the Point don't open their door to just anybody. Could be the cops wanting to ask nosy questions about a neighbour, some drunk looking to take a piss, or even the Jew. We just keep on eating. Mom makes us all drink a glass of milk, even though she knows I hate milk. I don't tell her but this milk actually tastes good. There's no lumps in it like the milk at school or St. Columba House. When I ask her why she isn't eating anything, she says she isn't hungry. She never eats anything. Nanny always says that's why she looks like a goddamn skeleton. Mom just smiles at me.

"I'll eat when my kids have grown up."

Chapter Five

JENNY QUINN HAS BLUE TOILET PAPER with flowers on it. Seriously. Toilet paper with blue fucking flowers. When I tell Annie she doesn't believe me at first. Not that I can blame her. Blue flowers on toilet paper? It's like wiping your ass with wrapping paper. I'm glad I knew to take a couple of squares to show her when I got home.

"It even smells like perfume?" says an amazed Annie.

We both lean in and sniff the squares again.

"You're right," says Annie. "Jenny is rich."

I've been saying Jenny is rich since she first became my best friend in kindergarten.

She gets her hair cut by a hairdresser, has a different white shirt to wear every day of the week, and the cake at her birthday party had money in it. After I bit down and found a nickel wrapped up in tin foil, I asked for two more pieces, please. Afterwards I went to the bathroom to pee and that's when I saw the toilet paper. There was even an extra roll stuck on a stick with a duck's head beside the toilet.

"No way," Annie says later. "What the fuck was with the duck's head?"

I hate it when I forget to bring some toilet paper home from school. The paper at school is real thin and you can see right through it, like the wings of a fly, but it's better than nothing.

Until I saw Jenny's scented blue toilet paper with flowers on it, the best toilet paper I'd ever seen was in the bathroom at Expo 67. I still remember the big dome filled with birds and all the tents with statues of people from different countries, dressed up in weird clothes. The Scandinavians were my favourite—the men looked just like nutcrackers. But it is the bathroom that I remember best. It was so new and clean. There weren't any cigarette butts clogging the sink or any pictures drawn on the stalls. It's the cleanest room I've ever been in. Not even Annie and her bottle of industrial strength cleaner could get our kitchen as clean as that bathroom. I almost forgot to use the toilet. I noticed there wasn't a lid on the toilet, just a seat. If a rat crawled up the pipes it wouldn't have to bang its head over and over until finally jumping out. I tried to imagine a rat crawling out of the toilet and running loose in that clean bathroom. I wondered if that's why all the toilets I've seen in the Point have lids—to keep the rats in. I could've lived the rest of my life in that bathroom.

When I told my friend Marsha about the dome and the tents and the bathroom, she asked how the hell my mom got any of us to the Expo. I have to admit I'm not exactly sure. Maybe Mom got some tickets from her commie friends. Or maybe it was just a dream. I told Marsha about how when we were on the metro, when I looked out the window there was a cartoon of Tweety Bird moving right along with the train.

"Yeah, you were dreaming," said Marsha.

When I tell Nanny about Jenny's fancy blue toilet paper with the flowers she says it's a sin.

"That is just an affront to the Lord," Nanny says. "Using the facilities to evacuate our bowels and bladder is meant to be a simple task, and already a luxury since only humans get to sit on a throne while they do so. Only a simpleton or a show off with too much money turns it into a public display of wastefulness."

I think Nanny is just jealous. She has a Two Squares Only rule at her place and reminds us every time we use her toilet.

"Don't you be using more than two squares!" she'll yell through the door.

After I tell Nanny that I think Jenny is rich, Nanny says there are only three kinds of people in the Point, and none of them are rich.

"First, there's the hard working Scottish and British. They aren't afraid to get their hands dirty just to make a few honest dollars and they aren't too proud to try and make a decent living for their families doing anything. Just as long as it's legal and doesn't offend the Lord in any way."

I know lots of those types. Some of them think me and my sisters are shit bags because we don't always wear socks and underwear.

"Then there's the Frenchies," says Nanny. She never calls them Peppers because she thinks that's low class. "They cluster together in little Pepsi pockets around the Point, though most of them are smart enough to know their place is in the north end."

I'm surprised to hear Nanny say Peppers are smart about anything. Most of the time she's going on and on about how dumb the French and their language are.

"Why say *mort*?" asks Nanny. "People don't *mort*, they die! And a window is not a *fenêtre*. The French language is just plain nonsense."

According to Nanny, some of them have jobs, though. But I can't tell which ones wear socks or underwear.

"And then there's the unemployed drunken Irish spread all throughout the Point," says Nanny, "starting all the Victoria Day bonfires."

That's the group my family is a part of but I've never started a bonfire anywhere in the Point on purpose and none of my sisters have, either. I think Jenny must be part of the Scottish and British group, like Nanny.

"If your grandfather hadn't liked his drink so much," Nanny often reminds us, "I'd be rolling in the dough. But money ran through that man's fingers like water. When he died he didn't leave behind anything but his debts. Not even two wooden nickels to rub together of insurance money."

I've heard the story about how Nanny's husband died at home about a hundred times. My dad was only twelve when his father died. Dad watched as his father got smaller and smaller every day because of the cancer wrecking his lungs.

"My father had been such a large man. So full of life. It was shocking to see him get so sick, shrinking right before my eyes," says Dad.

We've all seen the paper from the army about grandpa winning a medal for "splendid leadership and courage and conspicuous gallantry." Nanny likes to show it to us every once in a while. One time she laughed as she told us how afraid our dad had been after his father died since they kept his dead body in a coffin in their own living room.

"It was traditional back then to hold the wake at home," said Nanny, "with the body laid out for four full days. Your poor daddy kept having nightmares about his own father, saying he thought the dead body was creeping up the stairs each night! I had to remind him that his own father wouldn't hurt a hair on his body."

Poor Dad. That story always creeps me out every time I hear it. I don't know what I'd think if I ever had to sleep in the same house as a dead body, even the dead body of someone in my own family. Maybe that would be even worse. But I just smile at Nanny and nod, like I agree it was silly of my dad to be so afraid.

Sometimes when I'm in Nanny's bathroom I try to unroll four squares but she listens at the door for the sound of the paper rolling, so I have to pull it as slowly as possible. But I swear she has X-ray eyes and can see what I'm doing on the other side of the door.

"I know what you're doing, I hear you in there!" yells Nanny, and then bangs on the door. "Only two! Children don't need more than two squares for their business!"

When I come out I know how to distract her.

"Did you see Mom on the news yesterday?"

Nanny frowns.

"I don't understand why someone would want to be famous for being poor and having stupid children. I don't put no mind to people who try and blame the government or working people for their troubles."

Nanny isn't the only one who doesn't like seeing my mom get so much attention. At school one morning, one of the Lynch girls told me what she thought of my mom being on TV.

"Someone needs to tell your mother to mind her own fucking business and stop trying to tell the rest of us what we need to do..."

I didn't let her finish.

"Well if you ever grow the balls big enough to say that to my mom's face, I say go right ahead. But if you ever use the word 'fuck' in the same sentence when talking about my mom again, I'll punch your fucking head in."

Ruth and Annie stepped closer when one of the other Lynchs looked a little too interested in what I had to say.

"If it wasn't for my mom, the people with real brains would be stuck forever in the bobo classes at Lorne with you and the rest of your dumbass family."

Annie cleared her throat, then pretended to be speaking only to Ruth.

"Good thing the Lynchs are not only stupid, they also know when to shut the fuck up before they get into serious trouble."

The Lynchs aren't afraid of me but they know not to mess with Ruth and Annie. Especially not at the same time. Both of them are about the most fearless fighters on the planet. Ruth makes you think she's about to walk away and then suddenly turns back and rips your head off and hands it back to you. One time an older girl at Marguerite-Bourgeoys Park had me pinned and was trying to jab a dirty old Popsicle stick off the ground into my ear. I was frantic to get her off, shaking my head back and forth before she could stab my ear when suddenly she was airborne. A second later, Ruth had one foot planted solidly on the girl's throat, the other ready to kick her face in. That kid was going nowhere.

"Come on Kathy," Ruth says all calm-like, nodding at me. "Get over here and put some dirt into this filthy bitch's mouth. Come on!"

I looked away and Ruth decided to help me out and do it herself.

Annie is the bravest person I know, especially when someone's messing with a sister. One time I got cornered by a bunch of Peppers living at the end of Rozel Street and didn't know what the hell I was going to do. They were circling, speaking Franglais, and having some fun with me, pushing and shoving. My dad always says that if you're cornered and have no way out, at least give as good as you get. I had decided which kid I was going to take out when suddenly Annie was there, pulling on my arm and dragging me away. Once safely across the street, we gave them the double finger and then ran the rest of the way home, laughing. We agreed not to tell Ruth. She would have marched us both back.

"And teach the fuckers not to mess with any of us Dobsons!"

I know I'm lucky to have my sisters, Ruth and Annie. I can go almost anywhere in the English parts of the Point. Only an outsider, someone who doesn't know who my family is, would try to start something. Even the pervs get nervous if they find out it's a Dobson girl they paid a bag of chips to look at their dick and let them cop a quick feel. Everybody knows what happened to that guy on the end of Bourgeois Street who tried to touch my sister Julia's flat chest after she knocked on his door for the March of Dimes. My dad needed surgery to have his knuckles reattached and the perv needed a steel plate put in his head to keep all the parts together.

"Stop your father!" Mom yells to me.

Dad is heading out the door with his baseball bat, not saying a word. Julia is crying.

"No, Dad, no! It didn't hurt. I swear it didn't hurt!"

But Dad has already left, walking real fast towards the perv's place. I can hear Mom as I run behind him.

"See what you did? Do you want your father to go to jail? Do you want him in prison forever?"

When I finally catch up with Dad, he's already outside the perv's house. He's yelling, and getting louder.

"I said to open this door NOW!"

When Dad starts smashing the windows on the ground floor, one by one, a woman inside starts crying. Next Dad starts whacking at the door. It sounds like a gun going off. The wood starts to splinter.

"Dad, no!" I'm yelling but I know he can't hear me. I'm afraid to get too close. Glass is flying and the bat keeps moving.

The woman inside yells from behind the door, "No! Please, stop! Go away. He's not here. He's not home!"

Dad keeps hitting the door. The woman suddenly opens it. She's an old lady. Her hair is wrapped in a scarf. She's so old she can't stand up straight.

"Please, stop, I beg you! My son's a very bad man. He's not here, I swear he's not here!"

Dad suddenly drops the bat. I know he won't hurt her. He's always telling Uncle Patrick that it's wrong to beat on Aunt Olive. Dad says it's wrong for a man to hit a woman. For a boy to hit a girl.

"Never hit a woman with a closed fist, Pat," Dad would say. "You could really hurt them."

I touch Dad's arm and he looks down at me. He seems surprised to see me standing next to him.

"Look out for the broken glass, Kathy," he says then gently moves me back a few feet. We can both hear the police siren getting closer. The sidewalk has become very crowded. Dad looks around and everyone drops their eyes. No one has seen anything.

"Come on," says Dad. He bends over and picks up the bat, then takes my hand and we walk away. The old lady is crying. It would take a whole week before Dad would catch the perv, sneaking in through his back door. The old lady wasn't there to save him that time.

Mom is waiting at the front door when we get home. She looks like she's about to burst.

"What did you do?" she demands. "What did you do?"

Dad looks at Julia, both arms wrapped around her chest.

"Come here," he says.

With a sob, Julia moves towards his arms and when she reaches him, he lifts her up.

"I'm sorry, sweetie. I'm so sorry."

Dad looks at Mom over the top of Julia's head. "Nothing. He wasn't home."

He puts Julia down. "Next time you come and tell me right away, okay?"

Julia nods but I know she'll never tell Dad another thing about any of the pervs. She realizes now why none of us ever talk. Nobody wants Dad to go to jail forever.

Mom tells us to go play outside. Julia and I sit on the front stoop. We can hear them fighting inside.

"I'm sick of this," Mom says. "I can't live like this. You can't keep bringing this crap into our lives. You know the cops are going to come looking for you again, right? Not to mention all of your other friends. I'm tired of ducking and almost shitting myself every time a car backfires, a fucking bomb goes off, or someone knocks on the door."

"Oh, for Christ sake," Dad says. I'm shocked. He never swears. "No one is going to do anything to you or the kids. You know they don't work that way. You don't have to worry. I'll take care of it, you know I will."

Mom asks Dad if he's drunk again and even I can tell she doesn't really think he is. She asked the question just to be mean. Dad comes storming out a few seconds later.

Nanny always says that my dad learned to smoke and drink when he was seventeen in Korea, fighting the gooks and trying to save the world from commies with his best friend, Uncle Luther.

"Come on Russ, if you sign up we'll have a whole country to party in and no one to tell us what to do!"

Uncle Luther knew how to make my dad do stuff. Nanny says they grew up like brothers. Uncle Luther is his cousin.

"Think of all the girls, Russ!"

I think my dad is the most handsome man alive in Montréal. Not that dead people are much competition, but if you were to line up every man on the Island, everybody would agree that my dad is the winner. He looks exactly like Captain Kirk, only taller. My mom says his good looks are what get him into trouble. I'm not sure if she means my dad or Uncle Luther, who looks exactly like Elvis. Dad and Nanny both had to sign some papers for him to go to Korea and kill the gooks. She promised he already knew how to kill bad people, even if he was only seventeen, and he had to sign for them to send her all his money. Nanny has always worried a lot about money. Ever since her husband died, when Dad was only twelve, she's been real careful about how she spends it. Uncle

Luther didn't need his mother to sign any papers since he was older. I guess he got to keep all his money, too.

Dad never reads us any books like Mom does every night, but he still tells us stories. Sometimes he tells us about Korea. Some pretty gross stuff happened over there but Dad only talks about it after he's finished meeting with his friends at the Legion. He always tells his stories in the same order. First is the one about the Bren gun, a story I had to hear about a million times before I finally realized that Dad wasn't talking about a "bread" gun. It was a real gun, the Bren gun.

"We were sitting around trying to keep dry," says Dad. "There was a light drizzle and the ground was all mud. Our boots were filthy so we didn't want to take them off but some of us were cleaning our weapons."

I knew not to ask how a person cleans a gun. With soap and water? A special rag?

"Billy let me hold his Bren gun because he knew I'd give it a good once over before firing a couple rounds off. But before I could even unload it, suddenly shots were coming in from all sides. We hit the ground like we'd been struck and I immediately began crawling away from the group. We all knew you don't stay in a clump like that and let the gooks take you all out in one blast of glory. So I'm humping my ass as close to the ground as possible, hoping a gook doesn't hear that sucking noise the mud is making—so loud I'm sure my own mother can hear it all the way back to damn Montreal, when suddenly I hear Billy's voice, like a squeaky little girl…"

At this point Dad is laughing so hard, he can barely speak. This next part is always the funniest part. We all laugh right along with Dad, not getting the joke but knowing it must be good. Dad takes a big breath and then continues.

"Russell, my Bren gun… give me back my Bren gun! Russell? Come on, man, give it back! Give me back my BREN GUN. RUSSELL, PLEASE!"

Then the sound of angry bullets hitting a body, and Billy stops asking for his Bren gun. I want to ask Dad what angry bullets sound like, hitting a body. But he's not laughing anymore. We know to wait, without making a sound, while he lights and smokes a Player's Filter. He stares straight ahead, as if watching the movie of himself back in Korea. Sometimes he studies his cigarette pack, like he's trying to find something gone missing. Maybe he's reading the tiny words on the side. Maybe he's counting how many smokes he has left in the pack. Annie is the only one who dares to speak.

"You want a cup of tea, Dad?" Annie has the best smile in the family. You feel happy just for seeing that smile. Dad nearly always refuses.

"No thanks, Dear."

But it reminds him he has to go for a pee before telling the next story.

I wonder sometimes whether Nanny knows any of Dad's stories from Korea. I don't think so, but she hardly ever says anything about Dad. She has lots to say about my mom though.

"Some people are just getting too big for their britches," Nanny says and I know who she's talking about.

"Some people just don't know how lucky they are," she adds as she puts more water in the teapot on the stove.

Nanny must drink fifty cups of Red Rose a day. She has nearly the entire collection of tiny statues now. One comes in each box of tea bags. They're all lined up on the windowsill in the kitchen. My favourite is the small Humpty Dumpty, he has a nice happy smile. I guess he hasn't had his great fall yet.

I know Nanny has never liked my mom very much, even before Mom started hanging around the hippies and commies. When Dad first told Nanny he was going to marry my mom, Nanny wasn't exactly thrilled.

"Those Richardsons are all trash and everybody in Point St. Charles knows it!" said Nanny. "That father has branded each and every one of those girls. You know that, right? There's not a clean cherry in the bunch."

I think it was kind of mean for Nanny to be blaming the Richardsons for stuff that wasn't really their fault. Anybody can get lice and lots of folks in the Point have roaches, and if you don't have money to pay for soap and underwear and socks and all the stuff we never have either, whose fault is that? People turned their noses up at the Richardsons because Grandpa used to beat his kids and mess with his daughters but how was that the kids' fault? Grandma didn't do much to stop him either. My mom said one time that when her sisters would cry out too loudly, or if Grandpa made too much noise while he hurt them, Grandma would finally open her mouth.

"Edmund," she'd say, "come away now, leave the girls alone."

But maybe she should have gone into the room and kicked his scrawny ass, or taken the baseball bat he had broken one of his son's arms with to his mean old head. If you ask me, a cracked skull would have only been an improvement to that old bastard. But nobody is asking, nobody ever does. So that old prick got to drag his kids down in the gutter with him, covering them with his shit. But the stink was his alone. Even though Mom was a filthy Richardson, she was also known for being one of the most beautiful girls in the Point. Even Uncle Luther, who Dad says has been with more women than anyone can count, would tell Dad she's a looker and he'd be lucky to land her. Nanny finally let Dad marry her because she was the lesser of three evils between the gook and the used-up old bid.

Dad met Peanut, the gook, when he was in Korea. Dad says she was clean and funny and he wanted to bring her back to Canada and make her and their baby a Canadian. But Nanny says you can't make a gook into a Canadian, no matter how pure the seed from the father.

"It would be like trying to make silk out of a cow's ear."

I don't know why a cow would want silk ears but Nanny told Dad that she'd never be his mother again if he brought home his slanty-eyed yellow skinned concubine whore, and nobody wants to not have a mother. When Nanny asked him if Uncle Luther knew what he was planning, Dad said he never told Luther about her.

I bet Nanny's eyes got mean and tiny when she said, "You mean you didn't share your yellow rice-cracker with Luther? I thought you two shared everything?"

One time I snuck the picture out of Dad's Bible where he has tucked it between the pages. Peanut looks so little and pretty, I don't see any of the filth or ugliness or sin Nanny talks about. I think she looks happy, leaning against my dad in her dark blue dress with tiny white flowers stuck on the shoulders. Her long black hair hanging down, tucked behind her ears. I think we could be friends. He has one arm around her waist, pulling her towards him. They're both grinning at the camera…like they have a secret. I think she would have made a nice Canadian.

Dad had loved Emma Worth, the used-up old bid, for years and years, even before he went to Korea when he was seventeen. He even said one time that she was the woman who first taught him how to be a man, even after Nanny told Dad she was just white trash and had no proof that the bun in her oven was even his. But it wasn't her buns that Dad loved. At least I don't think so. He tells us that Emma was one of the kindest and most generous people he has ever met, would even give you the shirt off her back. According to Nanny, that means she was ugly as sin. Maybe Dad was trying to be fair to both Emma and Peanut when he decided to just marry Eileen Richardson, my mom, instead of having to choose between them. Nanny didn't like the idea of Dad marrying a Richardson, but she especially didn't want a slanty-eyed chink grandchild, and she definitely didn't want some used up old bid's kid, either. I guess Mom convinced Dad that what her father and brothers had done to her didn't really count, them being family and all, so he was finally allowed to marry her. In her only wedding picture, Mom is wearing a dark blue suit and a small hat, with a short veil that hides her eyes.

I'm not sure which one of my parents made the Rumpelstiltskin promise, but after their first-born arrived, they handed her over to Nanny. She was named Ruth Emma Dobson. "Ruth," for Nanny, whose first name is Ruth, too. And "Emma" for the used up old bid. Maybe that made it easier for my mom to give her away. She knew Ruth wasn't hers.

Now that Ruth is older she mostly lives with us, but she still visits Nanny on weekends and after school. I have lots of sisters but sometimes I think about my brother living in Korea, a place where they put shit on their rice to help make it grow faster. A slanty-eyed Captain Kirk. Only shorter.

I'm pretty sure Nanny has gotten used to the fact that my mom is a filthy Richardson, but she still isn't exactly her biggest fan.

"It doesn't help her hanging around with all those hussies," Nanny says. "I don't care how educated your mother claims those young women are. If they don't even have the sense, the common decency, to wear a bra and tame their lady parts, well then there's just no hope for them."

I know exactly who Nanny is talking about. Belinda Mavory. Like most people in the Point, Nanny has no use for social workers, but she especially despises Belinda. Mom has just come back from a meeting and it must have gone well because she's talking more than she usually does around Nanny.

"Thanks for babysitting the kids tonight," Mom says while Nanny puts on her hat and coat. "Tonight's meeting was a crucially important one. It gives me a lot of hope for the future. There are a lot of outsiders rooting for us and working hard behind the scenes."

Mom usually knows better but like I said, she's on kind of a high and just isn't paying attention like she usually does.

"Maybe we need a little less interference from outsiders and a little more attention on what's really important from the insiders," Nanny says. "Like their own children. I suppose that Belinda person was there tonight? I know how impressed you are with her, Eileen."

Nanny isn't paying close enough attention either. She misunderstands Mom's silence. It makes her bold.

"That woman really is a bad influence, Eileen, and like I was telling Russell just the other day, I think you need to limit the children's exposure to her and her kind."

Nanny has no clue what's coming.

"Her kind?" Mom says, all quiet like. "Her kind? Do you even have a clue what that young woman has done for us? What her 'kind' are still trying to achieve down here for all of us? She doesn't have to be here. She chooses to…"

Nanny finds her voice.

"How dare you speak to me like that. How dare you choose that sleazy slut over your own family!"

Nanny should never have called Belinda a sleazy slut.

"How dare me? How dare you! That so-called slut is going to change the world! Tell me what in the crying fuck are YOU ever going to do or change for the better, unless you plan to jump in front of a fucking Mac truck in the next twenty-four hours!"

I know Mom is going be mad at herself later for swearing like that in front of Nanny. It's the first time I've ever heard Mom talk that way to Nanny.

"Just wait until your husband hears about this," Nanny says, "speaking like white trash in front of a good Christian woman!" then slams the door behind her.

Mom calls Nanny an old fucking cow and other nasty stuff for over an hour after she leaves, banging stuff around the kitchen. But I know what she means. I want to tell her that Belinda said the same thing about her, that one day Mom would change the world. The week before, Belinda asked me and some of my sisters if we would like to spend the day with her.

"Would you guys like to go on a picnic?"

A picnic? Food in a basket, like on TV? I know the food will be shit. Belinda has funny ideas about what tastes good. Most of the commies and rich people do. A boiled egg wrapped up is still going to smell like shit when you unwrap it and I've never tasted a cold egg that didn't taste like a doll's head without the hair. But I know going anywhere with Belinda will be a fun. The day of our picnic, after first driving for a couple of hours in the rain, it finally starts to clear up.

"See? Now the sun is going to come out and we'll have a great time," says Belinda as she pulls into a large open field.

We all stand around the back of her car, holding our breath as we take tiny bites of the weird stuff Belinda had packed. Stinky eggs, icky cheese, sour pickles. I wonder how rich people eat this crap day in and day out?

"This candy is from China," says Belinda as she passes each of us what looks like a light green flying saucer. "See how clever it is? The wrapper is made of an edible substance. It doesn't stick to your hands and you can eat the whole thing!"

She's so happy with her gift of freaky candy from China, it would just be mean to tell her it tastes like cardboard. We're all still a little freaked out by how skinny she looked when she first got back from China. She says she was one of the first Canadian students allowed to visit, like that's a good thing. The sandwiches would have been okay except she made them out of brown bread and chopped up fish or something with even more boiled eggs. They smell like farts and mouse shit. The apple juice is great though. Belinda talks about her visit to China and how exciting it was to be part of the first group of students allowed in the country. She's so thrilled about the place, I'm secretly worried she might leave us all and move over there for good. I hate that we'll have to go home soon. I could listen to Belinda talk about China, or anything, all day. She makes everything sound like you're taking a walk through the scariest haunted house in the whole world, are scared shitless for most of it, but also proud when you finally make it safely to the other side. Then ready to try it all again. It's finally time to leave but the rain has started up again, soaking us all through.

"Oh no!" Belinda's car won't move. No matter how many times she turns the key or pushes on the pedals, it just won't go. After all the rain, it's stuck in the mud.

"Maybe we could try pushing it," says Belinda.

All us girls and Belinda try and try, pushing as hard as we can, but it's like the car is stuck in cement. Belinda takes us all with her to find a phone booth.

"We'll go back to the car and the tow truck will meet us there." I'm happy she isn't being crabby or making it seem like it's our fault at all.

"Sometimes things just happen that we have no control over," Belinda says.

"What's important is not why it happened, but how we deal with it. How we approach the problem."

She's so smart.

The tow truck seems to take forever but finally we see it pulling into the field and watch as it comes to a stop just a few feet from the car.

"What's the problem here?" asks the driver with a smirk.

He looks at his friend in the passenger seat and they both grin. "I see you girls are stuck pretty solid there."

Belinda's voice shakes a little when she says, "Unfortunately the ground was soft after the rain and my tires have sunk in pretty deep…"

"Don't you worry about a thing, doll face," says the smiling guy. "We'll have you girls all fixed up in a jiffy."

Somehow he managed to make 'jiffy' sound dirty. I don't like the way he and his friend keep looking at Belinda and then back at each other and grinning. They keep giving tips and making little speeches at us about what we should do in the future. I can tell Belinda is feeling bad. She's not smiling anymore and won't look at us.

"Maybe next time you little ladies might want to make sure you're on solid…"

Belinda finally snaps. "Don't you dare make this about gender. If you can't get my car out of this mud without making further comments then perhaps you need to leave and I'll call someone else for the job."

Me and the girls get so nervous we start giggling like idiots. These guys don't scare her one bit. Later I make myself believe that as we pulled away, the car finally free of the mud, I looked back at those two idiot guys, their mouths still hanging open, and yelled, "Assholes!"

Instead, me and my sisters just give them the finger as we pull away.

I want to tell Nanny that she's wrong about Mom. And Belinda. What Mom does sometimes is really scary and, like Belinda, I think she's fearless. Sometimes the police get really mad at her and sometimes they even grab her arm and pull her around. When the police show up at one of Mom's protests, a few days after our car trip with Belinda, they tell my mom and the other mothers that they have to leave the premises immediately. The mothers have been pretty loud, practically screaming while singing one of their favorite songs into their bullhorns, this one about the city's mayor.

"DRAPEAU IS AN ASSHOLE. HE SHALL BE REMOVED!"

When one of the policemen starts tapping his stick into his hand, Mom tells him they're demonstrating peacefully.

"We're just trying to bring awareness to a system which completely ignores the needs of our children. If any of your officers have children, I'm sure you understand what we're doing here is just for our…"

"I'm ordering you all to leave, immediately!" the policeman says in a very mad voice.

Mom looks at him all sad, like he's broken her heart or something.

"May I please recite 'The Poor People's Prayer' first, officer? Then we'll leave immediately."

Dad always says Mom is the master at making stuff up on the spot. The policeman hesitates for just a second, then nods and steps back. I can tell my mom is trying not to grin after most of the officers remove their helmets and bow their heads. Mom steps forward:

> Dear Lord, please look down upon us this day,
> As some of your poorest children at a moment of their
>   greatest need,
> And know how much we struggle and fight,
> For what we know in our hearts to be true.
> The right of our children to be equal and respected,
> And valued as all of your children, Lord.
> The right to warm clothing, a decent meal now and then,
> The love of their parents, and the protection from harm.
> The right to be treated as all children are, dear Lord,
> Across this wonderful city, the Island of Montréal, which
>   we all hold dear. Thank you Lord, for hearing our prayer

and helping us all to understand,
That the personal is political, and for giving the voiceless a voice.
And thank you for guiding the hearts of these brave and
    kind officers here
All around me today. Amen.

A few of the officers add their own 'Amens,' then put their helmets back on.

Chapter Six

DAD SAYS HE'S READY TO BECOME a card-carrying Communist. Mom got a job at the clinic and gets paid the same as the nurses, secretary, janitor, and all the doctors. At first Dad didn't believe her.

"No way! The same as the doctors?"

Dad says the doctors at the clinic aren't like real doctors anyway.

"They're just not normal. How much could they possibly be making?"

Mom shows him her pay stub and he sits down.

"It's only fair, Russ," Mom tells him. "That's why they sent me to McGill in the first place. That's what all those community organizer courses were about. It's all been about training me to give back to the community."

"Right," Dad says, "training you to become a professional agitator."

"Those courses just helped open my eyes even further," Mom says, "it helped politicize me. When I heard Bergeron speak at one of our classes, I learned about the real cause of poverty, the rip off of big business, and an awareness of the true enemy."

I know Dad wants to say something but he's still busy admiring Mom's pay stub. I'm dying to ask Mom who the real enemy is but I don't want to get kicked out of the kitchen.

"Now I want to block organize."

Dad looks up from the pay stub. "I don't even know what that means. Do you even know what that means? You've got a good job now, we can live like normal…"

"What's normal about our kids attending schools that are years behind the more affluent areas?" says Mom.

I wonder if Dad has noticed yet that Mom uses words like "affluent" and doesn't swear as much lately. She does when she's really mad or worked up about something, but ever since she started working at the clinic, it's like she's trying to use only her big words. Or maybe it's because of McGill. Mom tells us girls that it's one of the top universities in the world, so maybe she doesn't want them to regret ever letting her in. Mom is the first Richardson or Dobson to ever go to university. I'm going to be happy to be one of the first to graduate from high school. Mom made it to grade ten, which is why she knows so many big words. That, and she's always reading. Some people pick up accents from other people when they hang around them for too long. Mom steals their good words.

"Our kids are behind? How the hell can anyone even tell something like that?" Dad asks. "How can you even measure if a kid is behind another kid in a different school? Maybe Point kids just aren't as smart as the Westmount kids. You ever think of that?"

For a minute Mom's speechless. Then she forgets all about her new rule.

"Are you fucking crazy? You're saying that just to piss me off, right? We're talking about your kids here, your own kids. You know that, right?"

"I'm not talking about our kids," Dad says. "Our kids always get perfect report cards, I know that."

"Those perfect report cards are a lie, Russ, they're a lie! Lorne School loves that our kids know how to behave and not make waves. They don't tell their teachers to fuck off, they say please and thank you."

Dad is shaking his head. "Now you're the one selling our kids short. Every single one of them always has their face stuck in a book…"

"But not one of them can list the name of every province in Canada." Mom looks really angry now. "Not one of them knows their times tables, and not one of them can spell worth a shit. They don't even know the parts of speech."

The parts of speech? That isn't fair. Mom only knows that stuff because she's the one always making speeches.

"Our kids are ignorant of the most basic elementary…"

Dad looks over at me and asks, "Kathy, what's ten times eight?"

That's easy.

"Eighty."

Dad smiles at me.

"What's seven times eight?" asks Mom.

Now she's being mean. Nobody can get that one right off just like that, except for Annie, but Annie's a math freak. Dad's looking at me, smiling. I wish I could disappear. I'm worried he's going to think I'm picking sides.

"Annie knows her times tables," I say, not looking at Mom. "And Ruth does, too. I'm sure of it."

"You're sure of it?" Mom says with a mean smile. "I'm so glad you're sure of it."

Mom doesn't sound so glad to me. She's been taking all kinds of courses at McGill and they're making her even more crabby than usual. Every time she learns something new she comes home and looks at us like we've all become more stupid or something. I hate it when she asks me questions she already knows I don't know the answers to. Then I get to hear her on the phone with one of her new friends, bragging about how dumb I really am.

"She didn't have a clue! Doesn't know a noun from an adjective or a verb from an adverb."

Or my ass from my elbow.

Mom has also been taking French classes at McGill. I thought she already spoke pretty good French but she told us girls that she's learning how to speak educated French. Real French. Sometimes me or one of my sisters ask her to say Berri de Montigny metro, just to hurt ourselves. Her accent is so perfect, she doesn't sound like any Peppers I know from the Point.

"That's how they speak French in France," Ruth says.

Ruth's smart about stuff like that. She must read about a million books a week. One time she got hired to work part-time at the People's Library on Wellington Street. She got the job because of what Mom said was an Opportunities for Youth grant. It meant jobs for a whole bunch of really bossy kids like Ruth. She got to drink free Dr. Pepper all day while doing stuff she'd be thrilled to do for nothing. I wanted to do it too, for the Dr. Pepper. After a few days Ruth told us she was starting to hate Dr. Pepper but I think she was just showing off. I mean, who could ever hate Dr. Pepper? We were all proud and excited when the *Montreal Star* did a story about it in the paper and took a picture of Ruth to go with it.

"Library comes to Point St. Charles," the headline says. We all thought Ruth looked really pretty in the picture too, with her long hair in two pigtails. She wishes she had remembered to take off her glasses for the picture, but I told her they just made her look even smarter. And I meant it, too. She'd come home with all kinds of books nearly every day. Some of them smelt funny and some of them were missing the front cover but like Ruth said, as long as the words inside are still there and worth reading, who cares what the book looks like. Sometimes she let me and Annie and Julia hang around the library while she opened boxes and wrote stuff down on small pieces of cardboard in tiny print. We got to drink warm Dr. Peppers and look through the books, helping to pile up the really rough ones in one corner, and the ones that look almost perfect in another. Ruth told us the job would be hers until they got all the books out of all the boxes and organized onto the shelves. I told her she shouldn't work so hard and fast and she laughed and said the grant money would be finished by the end of the summer. Mom phoned everyone when Ruth was in the paper, asking if they had seen her picture.

"Doesn't she look great?"

Mom laughed at what Joe Bavota said in the article. He's one of the people in charge of the library. She read from the paper into the phone.

"He told the reporter that 'the people most interested in the library right now are the militant citizens groups. But I think that it will catch on.'"

Mom laughed again, then said, "Maybe if they didn't have that stupid three books for only two weeks rule they'd have more than just the speed-readers coming in for some books, too!"

Maybe it was because she worked there but Ruth got to bring home more than three books at a time. Mom said it was just a perk of the job and Ruth laughed. I've never seen Ruth happier. She bought herself a brand new pair of Dr. Scholl's sandals with her first paycheck. The next week she bought some jeans and underwear. She promised that she was going to buy something for the rest of us with her next paycheck.

Mom doesn't keep most of her own paychecks from the clinic. Every time she cashes one of her checks she gives almost half of it away before she even gets home. Some kids are sent by their mothers to wait for their fathers outside Northern Electric on payday, hoping to stop them from spending it all at the tavern before they get home. With Mom, if we don't meet her at the clinic on payday and beg her not to give it all away, she will. She really will.

"Of course I have to share this wealth," Mom says. "I can't keep all this for just us!"

Dad hasn't realized yet how much Mom is giving away. He's still stuck on the idea of her getting paid as much as the doctors.

"But doesn't it insult them?" he asks Mom. "Don't the doctors resent it?"

"Of course not!" Mom says, looking all offended. "These are not ordinary doctors, Russ. I told you, they're in this for the people. For them, it's not about personal gain or accumulating personal wealth. They understand that the contribution of each and every worker is equally critical to the overall success and smooth operation of the clinic. Of our entire community! How can you try and quantify the value of one human being over another?"

Dad laughs. "Seriously, you almost sound like you really mean it when you talk like that, Eileen. But it's me you're talking to, remember? Me."

Instead of getting mad again, Mom tells Dad how the Informed Citizens have been working towards this moment for years now.

"The clinic is like a fully equipped small hospital now," Mom says, and she's right. It has a waiting room, examination rooms, and all kinds of fancy equipment. It even has a psychiatrist.

"People won't have to leave the community now just to have access to decent health care," Mom starts ticking off fingers. "We have a well-baby clinic, nutrition classes with a dietitian, and even the diabetics can come to the clinic for regular monitoring and insulin shots."

She says "we" like she owns the clinic.

"I can't believe you commies have actually done it!" Dad says. "I admit it. I'm impressed."

Mom can even get credit now. A company has a special promotion going on that if you buy their huge fridge they'll deliver it fully stocked with free food. It takes three men to haul it up the stairs of our city housing apartment on the fourth floor. Mom hovers behind them the whole way up.

"Don't you dare scratch it!"

The men push it into a corner of the kitchen and then plug it in. My sisters and me watch as they quickly unload a whole mess of boxes. Ice cream, frozen corn, and hamburger patties fill the freezer. Then they put more food than I've ever seen all at once in my entire life into the fridge section. Milk, cheese, margarine, orange juice, eggs, hotdogs. I don't even know what some of the stuff is but I try to play it cool. Like we have huge food orders delivered once a week. That we drink milk and orange juice. And use real hot-dog buns with our hotdogs. After the men break up the empty boxes and finally leave, my sisters and me take turns opening and closing the fridge doors. I can't get over how beautiful it looks. So white. So big. I could hold the handles all day. Mom tells us not to get too attached to it, then asks who wants ice cream. We all laugh and scream and start yelling dibs. It's a race to the sink to claim the red bowl and best spoons.

"Hold on," Mom's smiling. I've never seen her looking so happy. "There's more than enough to go around."

The next day Sears delivers a brand new washer and dryer. Now I know we're rich. Really rich. No more having to drag all the dirty stuff down to the Quickie Laundromat in pillowcases to wait all day for a free machine. No more having to wear the same pair of pants to school for months and months until Mom can afford the quarter for the washer and a dime for the dryer. No more having Lucien, that cocked-eyed pervert who practically lives in the Laundromat, touching and sniffing our stuff and asking for hugs and for us to rub his shoulders. No more kisses tasting of cigarettes, stale beer, and rotten loose teeth. We now get to do our laundry at home and for free. Any time of the day. Any day of the week.

After the men leave, Annie starts making a huge pile of stuff on the floor in front of the machines.

"Mom? Can doing the laundry be my chore? Just me?"

It's like she's died and gone to heaven.

"Yeah, but you can't put any of that industrial strength crap in the machines."

Sears delivered the machines with a "Year's Supply of Free Soap." A year's supply? Well, maybe if you only do the laundry once a month and your family only has two people in it and one of them is a midget with really tiny clothes. But so what. The stuff comes for free with the machines. Ruth and me line up the boxes of free soap on the floor next to the dryer. I ask Mom if I can have a friend over after school tomorrow. I'm trying to decide who to invite over to show it all off to. Maybe Jenny? Or Marsha?

"You are not going to be a braggy little asshole," Mom says, "and show this shit off. Do you want the other kids to hate you?"

Annie has stripped all the bunk beds and pulled out the old sleeping bag that smells like cat shit from the box in the hallway. The huge mountain in front of the washer has now been organized into three tidy piles.

"That stuff doesn't even look dirty," Ruth says, eyeing Annie's work.

"Oh trust me," Annie says. "That stuff is filthy."

"Try not to break the machines their first day here, okay?" Mom says, looking a little worried.

"We gotta test run them," Annie says. "make sure we didn't get any duds."

Annie pulls the plastic off the instruction booklet, then tucks it under her arm. She goes off to have a crap.

Two weeks later when I come home from school the washer and dryer are gone.

"Did somebody steal them?" I ask Ruth.

"No," Annie says, trying not to look sad. "Mom gave them away."

She gave them away?

"What do you mean?" I ask. "Why did she give them away? Did Sears take them back?"

"No, it wasn't Sears," Ruth explains. "She gave them to the McDonald family over on Sebastopol."

"Why would she do that?" I don't get it. "Who are the McDonalds?"

Then I remember. That single mother with four kids living on one of the worst streets in the Point, one of Mom's newest families. She just started working with them a week ago. The two oldest kids have some rare disease that makes them age real fast. They're seven and nine but look like they're going on a hundred and a hundred and fifty, with balding heads, wrinkled skin, and aches and pains in their bones like somebody in a nursing home. They even have bedsores. Mom talked about them a lot after she met them for the first time and was upset when she learned from the doctors at the clinic that the disease these two kids have means they're going to die pretty soon. She told us how this mother is doing everything alone, without any support or money from anyone.

"She needs help," Mom said.

I didn't know she'd meant help from us.

"If not us, then who?" Ruth says. "Of course Mom gave her the washer and dryer. She says they need it more than us and she's right."

This mother had been dragging all four of her kids to the Quickie Laundromat whenever she had some quarters to do their laundry. I should have known Mom was going to find someone who needed the washer and dryer more than we did. I suddenly think of the fridge and run to the kitchen. Sure enough, a bare spot with some crumbs and dust are all that's left where the beautiful fridge had once been standing.

"They got our fridge, too?" I yell.

Annie follows me into the kitchen. "Naw. The bastards who own it came and got it. Said we didn't pay the weekly bill on the stupid thing."

"Did we get all the food out first?" I ask.

Annie points to a small box on the counter. "They stuck it all in there."

Some pickles, mustard and ketchup. And a jug of orange juice. Bastards. We aren't so rich anymore.

Mom says I'm lucky. All of us older girls are lucky. The three of us are going to start going to some fancy schools next week in Westmount. All the meetings, fist waving, sit-ins, protests, media crap and hard work have finally paid off. Mom smiles at the three of us.

"We've won!"

We're going to be the guinea pigs. I'm going to Westmount Park for the rest of grade six, and Ruth and Annie are going to Westmount High.

"They consistently have the highest test scores on the Island," Mom explains. "Their students always graduate from high school and many of them even go on to university. Forget about marrying a doctor one day, girls. You can become doctors yourselves!"

Who the hell ever wanted to marry a doctor? I want to be a writer. And I don't want any husband, ever.

"Who else from the Point will be going?" I ask Mom.

"A few other kids, including Jessica Murray," she says.

Jessica Murray? That little snob? She's only the most popular girl at Lorne School. Long curly hair, tight T-shirts, a steady boyfriend and big tits at twelve. In other words, I'm going to be at Westmount Park alone. All alone. I don't feel so lucky.

"They have a nursing program you can try to enroll in after you finish grade nine," Mom says, looking at Annie.

So much for becoming a doctor.

"Thank you so much!" Annie says.

I didn't know she wanted to be a nurse. I'd thought she wanted to be a vet or a germ killer or something like that. Maybe a researcher? An explorer? She'd make a good teacher. Half the shit I know and understand about anything is because Annie explained it to me. None of us would know how to play any board games if it wasn't for her. She always reads all the rules and shit and then explains it to the rest of us in normal words until we get it. I think she should teach stuff to stupid people. She'd be really good at that.

"What about me?" Ruth asks all hopeful.

"You'll be graduating from the top high school in Montréal!" Mom says.

Ruth has already done a year at the high school most of the Point kids go to and she didn't like it too much. I'm pretty sure Ruth wants to be an artist. She can draw anything. Animals, fairies, forests, people, anything. When we cut the models out of Nanny's Sear's catalogue to play with, Ruth draws us the men. Sometimes she makes them look like pirates and even gives them eye patches and furry chests. I watched how she did it one time and she made it look easy. Millions of tiny little circles all scrunched together until they looked like a real hairy chest. Then I tried it and knew it wasn't so easy. She sent in a drawing to a school that had an ad on the back of a magazine. It said if you could draw Sparky you could be a real artist, and they wrote her back a letter saying she was almost like a real artist already. None of us sisters were surprised one bit. Ruth's drawing of Sparky was so real, so perfect, it looked like she had taken a picture of the drawing and then just coloured it in. The art company on the back of the magazine must have thought so too because soon they were sending Ruth letters all the time, telling her how gifted she was and how a talent like hers was too strong and important to ignore and she was one of the few they were inviting to sign up for some of their art classes. Then she'd be as good as all of the other real drawers and painters, I guess. The ones that have their shit hanging up in museums and stuff. All she had to do was sign one paper and she'd be part of the special art school and never even have to leave our apartment. Imagine, a kid from the Point could be in a real art school and everything. But the more letters that came, the angrier Ruth seemed to get.

"It's just a rip off," Ruth said, tearing up the letters and putting them into the garbage.

Annie and me thought she should have framed that first letter, the one that came before they started asking for any money. The one that said she had a talent too important to ignore. Ruth decided to ignore the letters and one day they stopped coming. Ruth kept drawing Sparky though. In one drawing she had him wearing a fur coat, in another he was being fucked by Gentle Ben, that bear from TV. Maybe Ruth doesn't want to be an artist anymore.

Mom tells us we're going to love our new schools.

"They have the best teachers in the city, up-to-date textbooks, and the parents are all very involved in their children's education. I met with the principal at both schools and they're very supportive of the idea of integrating inner-city kids."

Inner-city kids?

"Do we have to wear uniforms?" I ask.

"No, they actually don't have uniforms, if you can believe it," Mom says. "They view uniforms as being oppressive and stifling individual freedom and choice, so they don't believe in them."

What's not to believe?

"How do we get there back and forth every day?" Ruth asks.

"Good question," Mom says with a smile.

Mom always says "good question" when she knows you aren't going to like the answer. It's to buy her some time.

"The school board has agreed to pay for your transportation. You'll each get free bus fare every day there and back."

Annie tries to still sound happy. "We'll be taking a city bus?"

Apparently we'll be taking the same bus together, only I'll be staying on it for five extra stops after Ruth and Annie get off. I'm glad we'll be on the bus together. At least for most of the ride. Mom says she's going to bring us over to the clothing room at St. Columba House for some clothes.

"You can't show up there looking like beggars."

The ladies at St. Columba act like we've won the lottery.

"Westmount is a lovely area," says one.

"I bet you're going to meet a lot of quality people there," says the other.

They smile at us a lot and spend a long time helping us find socks and underwear. Annie finds a skirt she loves and Ruth finds a pair of jeans. When they can't find any jeans to fit me, Mom says I can have Ruth's old pants.

The night before our first day, I find Annie crying in the bedroom.

"What's wrong?" I ask as I sit down next to her.

At first she won't say. Finally it comes.

"I don't have any pantyhose for nursing. You're supposed to wear white pantyhose for nursing classes and I don't have any."

Seeing Annie cry makes me want to punch something.

"Hey, they won't expect you to have the white panty hose right off the bat like that. Seriously, with you being new and all, they'll be too busy telling you all about their rules and shit they think is most important and I swear, the white pantyhose isn't going to be all that important to them on your first day."

I figure it wouldn't matter if I reminded Annie that she still has two more years to find, borrow, or steal some white fucking pantyhose. She has always been the type to worry about shit way in advance. It's why she's such a good student and is the one who'll actually make it into nursing school one day.

"And if it is important for some reason on the very first day, I say fuck 'em!"

Annie laughs and looks at me all hopeful.

"I'm not kidding, Annie. They'll be so busy oohing and ahhhing over the straight commendables on your report card, they won't give a shit what colour your damn legs are!"

Annie has practically had straight A's every year since grade one. She's the genius in the family. The next morning she's up an

117

hour before the rest of us so she can curl her hair. Nanny gave her a set of old hot curlers she didn't use anymore for Christmas the year before. Annie finally has her special reason to use them. I know it's going to be a special day when I see three bread bags lined up on the kitchen counter. Mom has made each of us a sugar sandwich for school.

"You need a lunch for your first day," she says with a huge smile.

I give her a hug then run to tell Ruth and Annie. Ruth is standing at the mirror over the dresser, pulling her long hair into a ponytail. Annie is making the bed.

"Mom's made us sandwiches for school!"

Mom yells that it's time to go. She makes each of us show her our bus tickets, then shoves us out the door.

"Come on guys, get moving or you'll miss the bus!"

As we walk to the bus stop, I can't stop talking.

"Mom says the Peppers and the English don't attack each other's schools in Westmount." I say. "They just stay at their own places!"

Ruth and Annie keep walking.

"Mom says kids don't even fight at the Westmount schools. Not ever, no matter what! Do you think that's true?"

Ruth looks at me like she's suddenly hearing me for the first time.

"What?"

I try again.

"Mom says the kids don't fight in Westmount. Not even with French kids. They never do any school invasions and they don't swear and Jenny Quinn says they don't have steady boyfriends until they're in grade nine and even then, they only do feel-ups and French kisses. No baggie explories or freebies even after six months! Do you think that's true?"

"What?" says Ruth with a grin. "No freebies even after six months? Why don't you call the president!" Her and Annie both laugh.

I had stayed up late the night before asking Mom a million questions. I would have kept asking her stuff all night until she finally told me to shut the fuck up and get to bed already.

"You'll be useless in the morning if you don't get some sleep. Trust me, you'll need your wits about you tomorrow."

Knowing I'd be in Westmount the next day made falling asleep impossible. Other kids in the Point had been coming up to me all week, asking me if it was true.

"Your mom is making you go to one of the fancy schools in Westmount? With the rich kids?"

I knew to act like it was a death sentence.

"Yeah, can you fucking believe it?"

But I'm thrilled. Even if only half the shit Mom has been promising me is true, I think I really am the luckiest kid in the whole world. Or at least the Point. In Westmount the kids will be nice and won't fight and, like me, really like school. Only they don't like it secretly. They can admit it right out in the open. And Westmount kids never get the strap. Not that I ever get the strap, and none of the girls I know in the Point get it either. But a lot of the boys do. After getting it two or three times, they're always mad at everything from then on, like they hate the world. The strap is the worst thing for a boy in the Point. It just ruins them. Makes them mean. But my mom told me that they don't dare strap the kids in Westmount.

"Their parents are all doctors and lawyers and educated people with money and influence. No one, least of all a public educator, would dare to raise a hand to any of their children."

I figure it isn't like they're going to know any different about me. As far as they know, I could be a real Westmount kid, too. I've been practicing saying stuff without swearing. You know, to sound like a real rich kid.

I say, "Excuse me? Pardon?" Instead of, "What the fuck? Are you nuts?"

Not that I ever swear around any of the grownups in the Point either, of course. They'd knock you off the side of the head if you tried pulling any rude shit like that. But Mom told us the kids in Westmount don't even swear around each other when no grownups are around.

"They're too polite and well-educated for that," Mom explained.

I can't wait to see who my new best friend is going to be. Some nice rich girl who lives in a beautiful house with important parents with lots of influence, who never fights or swears and eats breakfast and lunch and supper and even a snack sometimes before bed. I bet she even drinks milk. Mind you, I think milk is disgusting to be honest and only pretend to drink it when they hand it out at school on the free milk days. But it'll be okay if she likes it, she can have mine, too. I bet if she has a brother he won't be a perv in any way and I bet her uncles are even okay too. If she ever tells me her grandfather tries to stick his tongue in her mouth, I'll tell her what my cousin Lucy did when her father tried to sneak into bed with her.

"You ever try and touch me again, Dad," Lucy told him, "and I'll stab you with a knife right in your heart while you're sleeping."

Uncle Oscar never tried messing with her again after that. When I asked her what she would do if Uncle Eddy or Uncle Luther tried screwing with her she said she'd tell them the same thing.

"Touch me and I'll kill you. I'll stab you to death."

When Lucy lived with us for two years she always acted like she was one of us girls, like she was a real sister. Mom is always letting cousins with missing mothers move in with us. I tried not to hate Lucy and feel all jealous just because she has long beautiful red hair. Annie said it wouldn't be nice to hate someone whose mother had run off and left her behind. Even her report card said, "Absent Mother." Ruth hated her guts though. Lucy is a bit older than Ruth so I think they both wanted to be in charge, to be the boss. Lucy always treated me like a baby though instead of a sister or a friend, and told scary stories about Devil's Lane. Annie told me the stories were all bullshit though when she realized I was forcing myself to stay awake at night for as long as I could.

I bet my new best friend at Westmount High is going to love that I'll always have her back.

Me, Ruth and Annie are finally at the bus stop. Ruth looks at me. "What in the hell are you babbling about?" she asks.

Her and Annie are both staring at me. Their mouths are hanging open a little.

"God, there's no short cuts in your stories. You know not to talk any of that shit while you're at school today, right?" Annie says.

The bus pulls up and we get on.

When I say, "Good morning, sir!" to the bus driver and smile, he just looks away. Unfriendly fucker. I was going to tell him I'm not a retard, I'm just practicing my new Westmount attitude but decide to just follow my sisters to the back of the bus and sit down. Ruth and Annie still aren't saying much. Like they're sleeping with their eyes wide open. At first I check out the other people on the bus. Then I start looking out the window. It's weird how quickly the bus leaves the Point behind. Soon we're driving through downtown. The people getting on and off at Guy and St. Catherine Street all look like somebodies. Men with leather briefcases, women with makeup and haircuts you know they don't do at home themselves with scotch tape. Even the mothers with their babies look different somehow. A few kids get on and that's when I really can't help staring. I feel like I've landed on fucking Mars and I'm sitting in a small bubble that no one else can see. A bubble that lets me gawk and stare at everything and everyone, just checking stuff out.

Ruth leans towards Annie. "We're almost there," she says.

"Remember to wait five more stops and then get off," Ruth says, then pulls a string near the ceiling of the bus. It makes a soft dinging sound.

After they stand up and start moving towards the back door, Annie looks back and winks.

"It'll be great, Kathy. See ya later."

Her and Ruth both give me a big smile and get off the bus. Annie is lucky to have Ruth with her. Ruth isn't afraid of anything. She'll watch out for Annie, help keep her safe. I watch them through the window as they run across the street towards their new school. Westmount High looks huge. It's bigger than any building I've ever seen in my life. As long as two blocks in the Point. Maybe bigger. There must be five hundred or more students all wandering around the side of the school. Ruth and Annie quickly disappear into the crowd. My bus starts to move again. But now my stomach hurts, like feeling hungry and needing to take a shit at the same time. It feels like I'm in one of those movies where it shows somebody walking along the street all happy, not knowing that a werewolf is sneaking up behind them and is about to rip their face off. I look out the window again and press my forehead against the glass. There's lots of grass and trees. It's like seeing Marguerite-Bourgeoys Park, but with houses and apartment buildings sticking up all over the place. Westmount people get to live in a fucking park fulltime. I swear to God I must have seen fifteen squirrels in two minutes, running around the trees. People are walking dogs on leashes and there aren't any chip bags or cigarette butts anywhere. I start taking notes in my head for later to tell my younger sisters all about it when I get home. Westmount doesn't have any garbage and there's no stray dogs humping kids' legs anywhere. If you see a dog, you see a grown-up nearby closely attached. No cats wandering around either. At least not from what I can see on the bus. And lots and lots of squirrels. My stomach has stopped hurting. Just one more stop. When I pop up to pull the string, someone else does it before I can. A bunch of other kids get off the bus at the same stop. I want to say hello and maybe smile at them but no one is looking so I just move with them towards the school. I can't see the building yet but I know it's around the corner from the stop. A few seconds later, I see it. It looks like a fucking castle from one of the stories Mom read to us from Aesop's Fables. A small park in front of the school has green grass everywhere and even park benches. I can't see any chains attached to the picnic tables. Maybe they nailed the legs straight into the ground? Mom is right. None of the kids are wearing uniforms. They all have book bags though and they all seem to know each other. Mom told me to report to the office right away, that they'll be expecting me. I figure if I go through the front doors I'll find the office soon enough.

The secretary is nice but she seems to think I'm simple in the head or something. She keeps speaking to me in a slow voice, repeating herself like maybe I need to hear it all twice or I won't get it.

"How about if you sit yourself down right here young lady and we'll have your teacher come down and introduce himself, okay?"

I stare at my shoes while she says it all again. Maybe she's simple in the head.

"If you tell me which way to go I could just find the class on my own," I say.

Maybe she's like a record with a scratch and she'll just keep saying the same thing over and over again until somebody gives her a little push.

"Oh no, dear, we can't have you doing that!" she says like I just offered to go spray paint "Fuck you" on the walls.

"Mr. Levy will be along in a couple of minutes. You just wait right here."

Mr. Levy? A male teacher. Too bad. I think male teachers are usually icky or boring windbags. Or both. Like Dad always says, it takes a special kind of weirdo man to want to sit in a classroom with a bunch of strange kids all day that aren't even his own flesh and blood. Dad admits that his own children are the only ones he really likes. He's just being polite when he makes a fuss over somebody else's baby. Mom really is nuts about all kids though, especially babies. She just about loses her mind whenever she spots somebody on the street with a baby. She always has to stop and tell the mother that their baby is just so gorgeous and adorable and she can tell they're smart too, just from the way they're looking at her, all alert and stuff. By the time my mom is finished praising the baby, sometimes the mother will lean over the carriage and take a closer look, as if making sure she has the right baby stuck in there. But that's my mom. She's the only person in the whole Point who can keep a straight face while telling Judy Gagnon that her cockeyed twins are so sweet looking. Even I can tell Mom isn't lying when she says it. I have to stop myself from taking a second look while the mother is standing there, just to see if the twins are still staring off in four different directions. Dad calls it a gift, that only Mom can see the gold in all children. Even the cockeyed ones.

"Here's Kathy Dobson, your new student," the school secretary says.

I look up and my heart stops beating. Mr. Levy is the tallest man I've ever seen. He has dark hair, long for a man, but it doesn't make him look like a jerk trying to be cool or something. It suits him. I even like his glasses. You can tell he's smart. His smile makes me feel all weird and happier than I've ever felt in my life.

"Hello Kathy," he says then holds out his huge hand.

He expects me to touch him? I can't even speak. I feel so stupid and embarrassed, I stare at the hole in my shoe where my big toe is trying to come through then quickly look back up.

"Oh, she's a shy one," says the smiling secretary. I want to punch her right in the mouth.

"I'm not shy." I hope the old bitch finds the cord from the office phone suddenly wrapped around her scrawny neck the second she's alone.

Mr. Levy smiles. "That's great. Then why don't you follow me?"

Walking down the hall, I keep trying to think of something smart to say. Or funny. Or anything. But my mouth just won't work. I worry for a second that my feet will forget how to move and I'll be forced to crawl along the floor behind him, trying to pretend that's how I usually move around. I can feel my cheeks burning. Suddenly we're there, in front of the classroom door. It's open.

"Welcome to Westmount Park, Kathy," Mr. Levy says just outside the doorway. "We're really thrilled to have you join us."

Then he smiles again and I feel a bit dizzy. I follow him into the classroom. The kids are seated in rows and rows of matching desks and chairs. They all look up and stare at me.

"Hey guys, she's finally here. Let's welcome Kathy Dobson to our class!"

My sister Julia thought I was bullshitting when I told her later what happened next.

"No way!" Julia says. "You're making that up."

"I swear to god, on my life," I say. "The whole fucking class clapped! Like I was some movie star or something and they were fucking thrilled to see me there!"

Ruth and Annie don't say too much on the bus ride home but I don't think either of them are secretly wishing their teacher's wife will fall off a cliff or get hit by a bus so they can marry them instead one day.

"It's okay," Ruth says when I ask what she thinks of her new school.

"I haven't decided yet," says Annie when I ask her.

It seems wrong to say my school is the best school in the whole wide world when I can tell they're still figuring out what to think about their school. So I wait until me and Julia are alone before telling her how the floors are made of shiny wood that makes a nice and friendly creaky sound when you walk on them, and that the walls are clean and everything smells like oranges. I tell her how the bathroom doesn't have any shit on the toilet seats, and when I went for a pee during recess the sinks weren't all clogged up with wet toilet paper. I show her the roll I was able to take off in one clean shot and flatten, even with the cardboard still stuck inside.

"Nobody runs down the hallways or yells or talks when the teachers are talking. Teachers say stuff like, 'Pardon me?' and 'Would you like to give that another try?' and they don't interrupt kids, either. I swear it's like they really like being there or something. And did I tell you the stalls in the washroom don't have any writing on them at all? Nothing, I swear to god! And Mom's right, none of the kids swear."

I don't tell Julia that when I forgot and said "Shit" after I dropped my bread bag on the floor in the lunchroom, the whole place went completely silent. I can't imagine what would have happened if I'd said fuck. The kids sitting closest to me just stared for a second, and then started talking again like they hadn't heard me. After my face stopped being red and I could look up again, I saw one of them smiling at me so I smiled back. Her name is Alison and I bet we're going to be friends. Jessica Murray was in the lunchroom but she pretended not to see me so I ignored her right back. Bitch. Annie says she wants to reinvent herself, whatever the hell that means, so she's going to make new friends at the new school.

"You know the 'old' her and she wants to leave all that behind," Annie explains.

I show Julia the package of pencils, erasers, metal ruler, and pile of new notebooks Mr. Levy gave me. I let her pick a pencil and notebook out of the pile to keep.

"They were free!" I say, knowing I'm being all braggy now but powerless to stop.

When Mom gets home I talk nonstop until she tells me to take a breather.

"I'm glad they've created a nice and safe cocoon for you," Mom says. "They promised to make the transition as easy as possible. Mr. Levy is known for his genuine interest in the issues surrounding education for inner-city kids. He's one in a million. I wish we could shit out a hundred more like him."

Me too. It takes weeks before I can talk to him and use my normal voice when I do. At first I always sound like I need to swallow. It's so embarrassing. In the beginning, whenever he calls on me in class, I just shake my head or shrug my shoulders. Not that I ever know the answers to his questions. I don't. I can't believe how smart the rest of the class is. They're a bunch of freaky geniuses. They know what eight times nine is, what the capital of Canada is, and how to sing half of "O'Canada" in French. They even have ideas and opinions on shit I've never even thought of before.

"Can anyone tell me why it's inappropriate to water our lawns with city water?" asks Mr. Levy.

I'm fucking clueless. Gun to my head, or a million dollars if I get it right. Dead and poor. That would be me. Not a fucking clue. I wouldn't even be able to do my usual Dobson bullshit routine and make up an answer that, although sounding perfectly true, would be perfectly wrong. Don't water a lawn with city water? What other kind of water is there? And what exactly is a lawn, anyway? A rich person's word for fucking grass? Don't these people have better shit to think and worry about?

"It would be inappropriate," announces the kid behind me, "because you'd be using treated water. That makes it both wasteful and…"

Treated water? What in Christ's name does that mean? How'd these kids all learn that shit, anyway? Mom is right. Lorne School didn't teach us anything. Not that I'm sure what I'll do with all the stuff I'm learning at Westmount Park. Mr. Levy announces a project we'll be working on for the rest of the semester.

"I want each of you to invent your own country. You'll have to give it a name, describe its climate, geography, its people, culture, and what it imports and exports. I want you to spend some time researching and then after you decide all the five W's, I then want you to describe and share everything about your country. I want as many rich details as possible. You're going to put it all in a comprehensive report, then also make a brief presentation to the rest of the class. This is going to be exciting people, you'll each be inventing your very own worlds!"

Fuck me. All I can think about is getting home so I can tell Mom I need to transfer back to my old school as soon as possible. That, or find a bridge to jump off. Me, make a presentation in front of this class? A class filled with kids so smart they each know more than anybody else I've ever met, combined? Shit, they'll be inventing countries better than the ones that already exist. They'll be making countries so cool and awesome, other countries already here will want to change their names to the ones they'll be coming up with. How the fuck am I supposed to even try when I already know my project will be pure shit. Even the word "project" sounds too hard and fancy already.

When Mr. Levy says he wants me to stay behind for a minute when the bell rings for recess, I remind myself to breathe. Then I have to remind myself not to breathe too deeply or he'll think I'm a freak or something with my chest going up and down like I'm all out of breath. Fuck, that guy makes me a nervous wreck.

"Thanks for staying behind, Kathy," says Mr. Levy, like he honestly thinks I'm a kind and thoughtful person for agreeing to let him, my goddamn teacher, have a little talk with me. He's sitting on the edge of his desk. Man. He's so cool. I stare at my feet. My friends in the Point think I'm lying when I swear to them that none of the teachers at my new school have heard me say fuck or asshole or shithead even once.

"If you don't mind, I was hoping to work with you a bit on this project. I know it's a new challenge for you and since the other students here have already done lots of similar projects before, I feel they'd have an unfair advantage over you if I didn't provide some additional support. I know from your previous report cards that you're a hard working and excellent student with a positive attitude and great work ethic. I want to help you showcase your special skills here as well."

That's the nicest way anyone's ever said I'm a dumbass before. If it had been anyone else, I would have said "fuck you, too." I look up from my shoes.

"I've done lots of projects before," I say to Mr. Levy. I'm thrilled to hear my voice working normally. "Last year I did something almost exactly like this one. I don't know why it isn't on my old report card there but I guess it would give me an unfair advantage if I didn't tell you about it." I do a fake yawn and pretend not to know about covering my mouth.

Mr. Levy leaves his perch on the desk and sits behind it on his chair.

"I actually already did half of it in my head when you were talking about it to the class," I add. "I even have a name for it."

Please god, don't let him ask. I'll never scare my cousin Dennis again if you don't let him ask.

"Well that sounds great then," says Mr. Levy. He's frowning now. "Why don't you enjoy the rest of your recess now."

Fuck you, too. I leave the classroom and go outside.

Within a month I don't eat in the lunchroom anymore. It's too embarrassing to sit there at the long table with the other kids without a lunch, coming up with a different excuse every time one of them notices and asks me where my lunch is.

I forgot it. I ate it on the way to school. I knew I wouldn't be hungry at lunchtime. I hate lunch. None of your fucking business.

When Alison brings an extra bag one day and says it's for me, I have to stop myself from smashing it on the floor and stomping on it.

"I thought it would be, you know, fun if we ate the same stuff," she says with a smile.

"You are just fucking whacked," I say, then turn away from her hurt face.

She stops talking to me after that, but I don't care. She's forgotten about me now, just like the rest of them, and doesn't see me anymore. Now I usually sit outside in the park during lunchtime. I finally figured out what's off about the park. There's no smell. I didn't even know that cars have their own smell until I realized that it's missing here.

I thought no one noticed me missing from the lunchroom until one day Jessica Murray talks to me on the bus ride home. She waits until we're almost back in the Point.

"How come you aren't in the lunch room anymore?" she asks.

I have to be careful how I answer her. Jessica is just as popular at Westmount Park as she is in the Point and at Lorne School. She would be a powerful enemy.

Fuck that.

"Because something in there… smells bad."

The two boys from Weredale arrive a few days later. That morning, Mr. Levy makes an announcement to the class.

"Today we have two new students who will be joining us for the next month. They're residents of Weredale House."

Weredale? Fuck me. As in, 'Weredale Home for Wayward Boys'? Everybody knows that a 'wayward' boy is just a fancy way of saying a Juvie Hall reject. One baby step away from real jail time. Mr. Levy seems to think he's getting two new students we should all be feeling sorry for.

"They've faced and continue to face some real special challenges and I know all of you here will help me in supporting them and making them feel as welcomed as possible during their short stay with us."

I wonder what speech he gave about me.

We have a new student arriving tomorrow. I hope you'll all help me in making sure she never notices what a freak we all think she is. She's from Point St. Charles.

Maybe after the class gasped, he quickly added, "If we all clap enthusiastically when she steps into the class we'll mange to disarm her and make her weak. Within a few days she'll be tricked into thinking she's one of us. And one of us wouldn't hurt us, ever, right? So clap hard people and clap long. Let's make her think we're on her side."

I can't wait to tell Mom we're getting some criminals from Weredale House. Shit. Westmount Park Elementary is going to the fucking dogs.

Mr. Levy walks in with two rough looking boys behind him. One's tall and skinny, wearing tight jeans and a bandana with a hand buried deep in a back pocket. The other, shorter boy is heavier. Stocky but not fat. He has shoulder length curly hair. After Mr. Levy introduces them, they both look up and take a slow look around the room.

"Hey," says the shorter one.

"Yeah," says the other. His eyes stop on me.

I stare back for a second, then look away. Shit. We're going to have a problem.

During Independent Reading period, I'm so deep into my English class book, *Lord of The Flies*, I don't register the itchy spot at first. I scratch the back of my head, then rub the suddenly itchy spot on the side of my forehead. That's when I notice it. A louse. A single louse has fallen out of my hair and is now lying next to a period in my book. The period is bigger but the period isn't moving. Shit. I sit there, like I'm flash frozen, for the next ten minutes. My lungs finally force me to take a deep breath. Fuck. I have lice. Again.

The other kids are already starting to look at me a little funny. This is all I need to become completely invisible. I swallow hard. It feels like something is pushing on my eyeballs from the inside. I'm hypnotized by that small wiggling dot. I use my thumbnail and crush it on the page. The tiny corpse makes a small red spot.

"Are you okay?" Mr. Levy is standing next to me. He says it so softly, I nearly jump out of my seat. His face makes me want to start crying. I shake my head and turn the page. Please don't let him see what I just did. Please don't let him know what I have.

"Would you please stay behind for just a minute during recess?" He isn't asking. He's telling.

The rest of the period seems to take years. Whenever I see Mr. Levy looking over at me I pretend to be reading my book again, turning the pages, and making faces like I'm reacting to what I've just read.

Oh, how tragic. Poor Piggy is running away and his glasses have been broken. Must be so hard for him to see. Oh no, now they are planning to kill him. How sad. Thank god the bell finally rings. I stay in my seat, staring down at my book. I see Mr. Levy's shoes standing next to my desk. I close the book and look up. God, I wish so much I didn't love him.

"I want you to know that I'm always here for you, Kathy. No matter what. You can always come to me with anything. I want to help you."

I have lice, Mr. Levy. Creepy, disgusting lice. They live on my hair shaft, shitting out hundreds of tiny white eggs each day. Then their offspring, the little fuckers, come out of their shells and suck my blood, making my head itch like a bitch. The only cure is a special shampoo that not only costs a fortune, but is a pain in the ass to use cause we have to do the whole family at once. It would take most of my mom's paycheck to buy the shit, even if I'd be willing to ask for it at the pharmacy, which I'm not. Still want to help me? Wait a minute, did you just take three steps back?

"Thank you, sir. I appreciate your support. But everything is fine."

Mr. Levy looks sad. I try to think up some other disaster to lay claim to, something that won't make him hate me and wanna kick me out of his class. I can't think fast enough.

"Really, sir. It's okay."

Mr. Levy pulls one of the chairs over from a student's desk and sits down next to me. I instantly pull a few feet away, then feel bad. He has such a strange look on his face. I worry he thinks I was pulling away from him because he has bad breath or something. He quickly stands up.

"I'm sorry Kathy, I didn't mean to get all into your business and make you uncomfortable. I just feel frustrated sometimes because I honestly believe I can help you if you'd just let me in."

I clench my teeth hard. I can't look at him.

"Just know that I'm here, okay?"

Fuck. Why can't I have something good, like cancer?

Chapter Seven

IF YOU FALL DOWN AND THE ROACHES start walking over you the worst thing to do is try and run. I'm standing outside the abandoned building on Liverpool Street right across from where Nanny lives. Ever since the family that used to live there moved out the roaches have taken over the building. They don't even bother to hide anymore when you turn on the lights. The ones on the ceiling in the kitchen look like a large wiggling carpet. There are thousands of them up there but they move like one giant roach, all together, like they're sending out messages to each other. A bunch of other kids from the area have started hanging outside the building each night, too. We take turns shining the flashlight at the clumps of roaches as they spill out of the building at dusk to march across the street. It reminds me of playing with the mercury from a thermometer—rolling it up into a silvery ball, smashing it onto the sidewalk in a million pieces, and then starting all over again.

We dare each other to run through the house. Usually roaches hide behind a calendar or inside a crack in the ceiling, but in the abandoned house the roaches have nowhere to hide and are everywhere: clusters on the walls, the ceiling, even the floor. These aren't your normal cockroaches. These ones are fearless. Nanny says they're straight from hell.

"Tiny imps from the Whoremaster himself, carrying his message of possession and evil."

When enough roaches are gathered together in a small space, there's a strong smell of shit that comes off them. There's an unspoken rule about not knocking each other over, even as a joke, once we're inside. I'm afraid to even speak so I pretend I'm just busy concentrating. Cockroaches make a place seem colder, like they're stealing all the warmth or something. As we creep down the hallway towards the kitchen a few kids always chicken out. They don't say anything; they'll just suddenly freeze and not be able to take another step. It's like they've just realized what they're doing and can't stand it anymore. Sometimes they lose it and then you have to backtrack and help the jerk get out. Otherwise you'll have to listen to them scream the whole time until you're finished and ready to leave yourself. Mom keeps warning us to stay far away from the place.

"That fire trap is going to fall down the rest of the way any day now," says Mom. "If one of those old beams fall on you you're finished!"

I want to tell Mom that there are worse things than a falling beam. Like falling yourself. Most of the kids exploring with me already know that you have to stay real still if you do fall down, even if there's a puddle of roaches squirming towards you. If you don't move they'll just crawl right over you. But if you start screaming and waving your arms around and running they'll get confused and scuttle all over your body.

"The compass in their head gets all screwed up," Annie explained to me once. She knows about that kind of stuff- compasses and directions and north and south. One time she tried to explain how east is always to the right of north, followed by south and then west.

"Just remember: 'Never Eat Shredded Wheat.'"

"Why not just remember, 'North, East, South, West'?" I asked.

But Annie is always coming up with weird ways to remember stuff. Why not just remember what you're supposed to remember, instead of remembering something to help you remember? It's just an extra step. Of course, I've already forgotten what order the directions go in. I bet Annie still remembers. It's too bad you can't teach roaches about 'Never Eat Shredded Wheat' so they'll never get lost on your body and run all over your face. Instead you just have to lay still and wait for the roaches to pass over you. But I can understand why Jamie Moore always screams his head off and runs out of the house, roaches scrambling all over his body. It's so hard to lay still when roaches are walking over you.

After dark each night the roaches leave the old house and scurry in every direction, some of them climbing the bricks of neighbouring houses.

"I'm surprised the landlord isn't doing something," says Dad. "Nobody can move in until those roaches are gone, and those roaches sure aren't paying rent."

"That landlord is never going to do anything," says Mom. "He probably lives in fucking Westmount. He never fixes the broken windows, the pipes, or anything else in any of his other rentals, so why would he care about the roaches? The city needs to do something, though. They're spreading into other buildings and carrying their filth and disease with them. It's a goddamn fucking health hazard."

Mom read an article in the newspaper about the roaches. Now they're famous roaches. Some expert from a college said in the *Gazette* that he'd never heard of roaches moving in large groups.

"That expert should go stick his head in the house on Liverpool," says Mom. "He'll learn something new for sure."

I don't think that would be a good idea. Everyone knows about the city inspector who went inside the house. People had complained to the police about the thousands of roaches walking down the street and up the sides of buildings every night, and after Mr. Gillan actually shot a couple of the roaches with his .22, the city finally sent some people to kill all the roaches. But the city inspector walked into the house first, and 2,000 roaches fell on him like rain. A reporter from the *Gazette* asked Mrs. Martin about it since she lives so close. She said they had to give the poor guy a shot of something to calm his nerves. There was even an article about the roaches in a newspaper in Calgary, which said, "This is Cockroach Country." The article said how the inspector was "inundated" by the roaches, and I asked Annie what that meant.

" 'Inundated' is when a doctor puts a needle in your ass. So you won't get sick," said Annie.

I ask Nanny how she's going to make sure none of the roaches get mixed up with hers when they come visiting each night, and she shows me her can of poison stuff that she sprays in all the cracks and dark parts of her apartment, including behind the sofa and the back of the stove. That stuff makes you cough and your eyes water so I guess the roaches don't like it too much either. Nanny says the city better fix the problem soon or maybe the Queen's birthday will solve the roach infestation across the street from her place. Every Victoria Day the Point almost burns to the ground. People go crazy with firecrackers, sparklers, burning shitbags, and homemade firebombs. Anyone who owns a car doesn't leave it on the street, because they know it'll get torched or at least turned over. If they can't hide their car or drive it out of the Point and leave it somewhere safe, they surround it with friends and family members after sunset. Somebody always melts off their eyebrows or blows a couple fingers off while trying to set a shed or alley cat on fire. The problem with a cat is that it doesn't sit still like a car or a shed and once it's on fire it runs all over the place. One time my sisters and me saw a cat with firecrackers strung all down its tail. They were popping like gunshots every couple of seconds and the cat was trying to run away from its own tail. We chased the cat down a couple of alleys so we could pull the firecrackers off but it kept running away from us. Maybe it thought we were the ones who put the firecrackers on its tail.

I always feel uneasy when I see Jamie and Spencer making glass cherry bombs. The whole thing looks greasy, like it could all leak out in one huge puddle and stick to their hands and clothes. Every time they light the wick and toss one under a parked car, I hold my hands over my ears and turn away, convinced the car is going to blow into a million little pieces, with flaming tires flying through the air and tiny shards of windshield scattering in the wind. Instead it just makes a small lake of fire underneath. Jamie and Spencer laugh when I finally open my eyes.

"What the fuck is your problem?" laughs Jamie.

Sometimes the police show up and try to stop the burning, and we throw firecrackers at their feet.

"You little punks! I'll get you good!" they shout as we race back up the street.

"Fuck you! *Mange de la merde!*" we yell back.

"Hey, *ferme ta gueule, toi-là*."

Some of the older kids throw firecrackers into the police cruisers or pour gasoline over the parked cars and make a huge fire. My sisters and me only throw firecrackers on the street. And we never stick them on cats. This one time, when the police officers moved into the crowd and tried to stop the bonfire, some of them got hurt really bad. A couple of the firebomb throwers and gasoline pourers got arrested.

"Christ, those lunatics really went wild this year," Mom says every year while reading the newspaper out loud. She tells us how many arrests were made, how many police officers were injured, who blew off their fingers. We all laugh when she says a reporter from the *Gazette* had his car vandalized and she gets mad at us.

"The press needs to be safe!" she says with a red face.

I want to tell her that most of the reporters make us all sound like assholes in the newspapers, and if they aren't smart enough to leave their car at home on Victoria Day, maybe they aren't smart enough to write stories about the Point.

Mom always reads the saddest stories from the newspaper out loud. Any time a kid is hit by a car or drowns in a river, Mom finds the article in the newspaper and reads it out loud, shaking her head slowly and pausing every couple of seconds. Me and my sisters think she must like being sad. I think her secret wish is for one of us to die. Then she could be the one in the newspaper, the crying mother whose child drowned or was mauled to death by a bunch of dogs, the mother everyone in the Point would give sad looks to every time she walked by.

"You guys aren't going anywhere this year," says Mom every Victoria Day. "I want you all in the house before it's dark. I don't need to sit in the ER at the Children's all night when one of you blows off a fucking finger or goes blind from somebody's plan going wrong."

Mom is talking about the time that kid was caught by the guy over on Ryde Street. He was stapling a mouse to the guy's door handle by its tail when didn't the door suddenly open. The guy pulled the kid inside and beat the shit out of him before kicking him in the ass and tossing him back out. Kevin says the guy also shoved the mouse down the kid's throat and made him eat it but I think that part of the story is probably wrong. I mean, who could be that sick? But I know Mom doesn't want us being part of the group the police might decide to bang up a bit when they get fed up with not being able to do anything. Most of the time they just drive around in their patrol cars slowly, sometimes yelling stuff out their window. But every once in a while a younger cop, maybe new to the force, will get so pissed off by the firecrackers going off in his face or the bags of shit bouncing off his car door, he'll actually jump out and start chasing. Those are the best kinds of races. New cops don't know the back alleys and laneways in the Point like some of the older ones, they don't know which sheds are unlocked and which city housing blocks you can dash into and hide in the laundry room in the basement. But Mom still worries that one of us might get unlucky when one of the cops, especially one of the older ones, does get lucky and manages to grab a couple of kids. Then the pricks like to smack you off the side of the head a few times, shoving you around and asking you what the fuck is wrong with you and maybe they should stick your sorry ass in their squad car and make you sit the night out. Usually they'll just end their lecture with a kick to the ass and send you on your way. Then once you get safely back across the street you can start yelling back to them what a fucked up piece of burnt pig they are and how your uncle is fucking their mother and their wife is giving your father a blow job. Then the chase is back on and sometimes you can get two more rounds in before they finally get dragged away by their partner, telling them it's not worth it and to calm down because the little fuckers will just mess with them all night. But most of the time the police are too busy watching the fires.

Even if the whole Point burned to the ground I think Mr. Duffy's variety store on the corner of Liverpool and Coleraine would still be standing. Nobody ever throws firebombs or rocks through the windows of Duffy's Variety. It's like there's a shield around the place or something. None of the other corner stores, pizzerias, or pool halls have a shield around them, though. The owners have to stand on the sidewalk for the whole night once it gets dark and glare and shout at anybody who gets too close.

"You little shithead, I see what you're holding! Don't you even fucking think about throwing that!"

One time I asked Uncle Patrick why there's a shield around Mr. Duffy's place. Uncle Patrick lives just around the corner from Duffy's Variety so he shops there all the time. Uncle Patrick didn't answer right away.

"Some shields are invisible," he finally said. "And sometimes those can be the most powerful."

Mom doesn't buy anything from Mr. Duffy, but it's not because he's a Pepper. It's because he's not from the Point.

"If I spend money at a store I want it to go into the pocket of someone who lives in the Point. He's an Outsider," she says.

Maybe she's just mad because she knows Mr. Duffy would never give us credit for the month, anyway. Nanny says he only lets someone run up a bill if they're an Honest Person and a Tax Payer.

"He's a hard working Frenchie, that Mr. Duffy. He's at the store 16 hours a day, every day of the week," she always says.

Nanny says the Lord won't hold it against Mr. Duffy for working on Sunday's because the Lord knows the hardest working people in the Point need him. Every time Nanny buys something from the store, Mr. Duffy writes down the price in the little book he keeps in a drawer under the cash register, and then he writes the same thing in Nanny's copy of the book. At the end of the month Nanny gives Mr. Duffy her government check and after adding up all the prices in his book, he gives her the change, which she uses to pay her rent and all her other bills. You can buy almost anything at Duffy's Variety, and if you can't find something you want, all you have to do is show him a picture from a catalogue.

"Uh huh, okay," he'll say, scribbling in his small notebook.

One time when Nanny got her check from the government it

wasn't enough for the food bill. Me and Annie watched her flip through her grocery book, running her finger along the prices and shaking her head. She must have added up those columns five times and each time got the same amount.

"What am I going to do?" she said but I knew she wasn't asking me or Annie.

She scared me a little when she started crying. I had never seen her cry before.

"What am I going to do?" she said a second time, looking at the numbers she had written at the bottom again.

"Don't worry Nanny, we'll just explain it to Mr. Duffy," Annie said. "We'll explain how there was just a stupid mix up, and how those idiots didn't send you all the money they were supposed to. And when you get your next check, you'll pay the balance for this month along with next month's."

Nanny looked over at us. "You think so?"

"I know so!" said Annie. "Yeah, come on. I'll go over with you right now and we can explain it all to him, okay?"

Nanny put her face in her hands and started to cry again. Annie went to her immediately.

"Nanny, I'll go myself. You want me to go? I'll explain it all to him for you, I swear. He knows you're a fine and honest Christian woman. He won't be mad or mean or anything at all. He knows you're good for it, honest he does."

Nanny reached up and pulled Annie's hand to her face and kissed it. I had to look away.

"You are such a sweetheart," she said in a voice I didn't recognize. "It'll be okay. You're right."

Then she stood up and walked over to the stove and grabbed the teapot.

"Who wants some tea?" she asked.

Her face was still red and wet looking and I wanted to go home more than anything else in the whole wide world but Annie was nodding at me behind Nanny's back and I knew she'd kill me later if I didn't say yes.

"Thanks Nanny!"

We both choked back two cups before Annie must have felt it was okay to finally leave.

"We better get home before Mom is looking for us," said Annie. Nanny hugged her a long time and then nodded at me.

"Let me know, Nanny," said Annie. "You just let me know."

Nanny's face looked like she was going to start crying again as we quickly went down the stairs.

Mom says she's going over to Margie's place. Margie Wallace is Mom's best friend in the Point and if she's going over there it probably means her whole gang is going to be there as well, and that means she'll be late. Once her and Margie, Anita, Vivian and Terry get together that's it. I've never heard five women with so much to say. Mom always says with her gang she can do anything. She doesn't mean beat the crap out of people or set a shed on fire. She means they can bash men and explain to each other over and over again until they each understand it exactly why men are such assholes and why they don't need them and why they hate them and why they're pretty much the most useless kind of human beings on the planet. Sometimes Mom embarrasses me in front of her gang, though.

"Look at this," Mom says to her friends.

They're all sitting around the kitchen table drinking coffee and smoking when she suddenly holds up one of my letters.

"Mom, don't!" I try to grab for the letter but she turns her back to me and holds it up higher.

"Here's proof of how smart my kid is," says Mom. She's laughing so hard now she can barely speak. "She not only writes me letters from camp, she writes them before she even gets there!"

She must have gone through the garbage bag I had all packed up for camp and found the letters. I thought I was being pretty smart to do them in advance like that because I know once I get to Camp Amy Molson, the last thing I wanna be doing is writing some letter when I can be swimming in the lake, making crafty shit in the Arts and Crafts building, or walking along the waterfall trail looking for Jelly Bean Lookout so I can peel the white bark off trees to bring home as proof to all the kids in the Point who don't believe me when I say that paper really does come from trees.

Mom's gang is all looking at me now. Terry and Anita are laughing. Margie is smiling at me. Vivian looks away.

"Dear Mom, camp is going great and I'm having lots of fun…."

I run out of the kitchen and go outside. Fuck. I hate my mother. I love Camp Amy Molson though. Even though the food is weird sometimes, you're never hungry at Camp Amy Molson. They give us breakfast, lunch, supper, a snack in the afternoon from the Tuck Shop and then a snack again before we go to bed, and it's all for free. The first summer I went there with Ruth and Annie I couldn't believe how much food they put on every single table for all the different cabins. I hid a piece of toast in each of my pockets to share with my sisters after our first breakfast. When I finally got to see them later in the camp's big playground, they showed me they had stuffed some toast into their pockets, too. We ate our toast as we watched the other kids climb the huge monkey bars and go down the slides. I liked how salty the butter tasted. When it's lunchtime we're allowed to eat as many hotdogs as we want. Although they don't serve some of my favourite stuff, like Point Pogos, which is a couple of French fries rolled up inside a slice of bologna, they give us peanut butter sandwiches, potatoes, and every single Sunday we get chocolate cake and ice cream for dessert. It was at Camp Amy Molson that I got to eat a whole bunch of stuff for the first time, too. Some of it was weird, and some of it was gross. Like raisin pie. Who fucks up a perfectly delicious pie shell by cooking raisins in it? The first time it came to our cabin's table in the dining room, I was all excited. We already had blueberry and apple pie, and I could hardly wait to see what kind this one was.

"Ah, raisin pie," said Miss Karen as she sliced into it, dividing it into equal slices for each of us.

As soon as I saw that limp looking wedge on my plate, the cooked raisins slightly burst and swollen looking lying inside a brown sauce, I swallowed hard. Baked roaches. That's what it looked like to me.

"No thanks," I said and pushed my plate away.

Miss Karen wasn't ever mean or crabby if any of us didn't want to eat anything. As long as it wasn't seconds you had asked for and then decided you were full, she was fine about you not wanting to eat stuff. Poor Annie though had Miss Christa. Miss Christa was big on making her campers try everything at least once. She told Annie she'd never know if she really liked something if she didn't at least give it a try and always made her campers take a couple of huge bites of everything before she'd allow them to stop eating whatever it was they didn't want to eat. Sure enough, after pushing away my plate of icky looking roach pie, I heard the dry heaving. Annie's cabin had its table just a few over from mine. I looked over just in time to see Annie leaning away from the bench she was sitting on, puking up those two or three bites I guess Miss Christa had forced her to choke down, followed by the four hotdogs Annie had eaten first. That pie was gross but the weirdest thing I've ever had at Camp Amy Molson is shepherd's pie. Calling it a pie seems like a cheat. The mashed potatoes covering the disgusting stuff hiding underneath are okay. I learned how to eat just the top and avoid the cat puke called creamed corn sitting on top of minced meat. It was too bad about the meat. If I could have picked out all that messy corn crap I probably would have liked that, too. After we'd finish eating, sometimes the camp director Mrs. Rogers would sit at the piano in the corner of the dining room and sing while she played. I knew it would be rude to do anything but listen all politely but sometimes I'd have to pretend I was tying my shoe laces over and over again so nobody could see me laughing.

"Summertiiiiime...in the city," she'd sing in this really high-pitched voice that Mom later told me was opera.

"Wealthy people really enjoy opera," explained Mom.

I don't know who the wealthy people at Camp Amy Molson were but my favourite songs were the ones the counselors taught us to sing along with them. Sometimes we'd have singsongs with the whole camp at a huge campfire on the upper compound, singing, "She'll be coming around the mountain" and "They built the ship *Titanic*." Sometimes we'd roast marshmallows and I'd get to sit with Ruth and Annie and we'd cook our marshmallows together. Eventually Julia would come to camp, and then Beth and Hannah too when Mom worked in the kitchen one summer.

I can still hear Mom and her gang laughing in the house at my letters from camp. Bitch.

I've been learning how to smoke. I practice in the bathroom at home but I still end up choking and coughing sometimes. I know it's a trick that I still have to learn, how to hold the cloud of smoke inside my body without it trying to force its way out until I let it. Annie found my pack of Player's in the bag under the sink and she drew a small skull and crossbones on the inside flap.

The two boys from Weredale, Gary and Bryan, already know how to smoke. I hang out behind the back of the school with them during lunch while they brag about how tough they are and tell lies about how many people they've killed and the bombs they're planning to set off in the metro.

"People are gonna shit when they see fucking Guy Street going up like a fucking hot cocktail," says Gary.

He's all talk though. I bet he's never even seen a firebomb go off, otherwise he'd already know they aren't big enough to blow up the metro. I've seen plenty of firebombs chucked at cars on Victoria Day, but they never make a big explosion. The fire slowly spreads from the bottom and the car silently burns for a while. Although he likes to play at being some dangerous kind of tough guy or something he's only in Weredale because his father almost killed him during his last beating and he ended up in the hospital with two broken arms and a crack in his cheekbone. They sent his father away for a while after that, even though Gary tried telling them he had fallen down the basement steps. Gary says his mother gave up on him, saying he was out of control after he refused to go to school and he smacked her and told her to shut the fuck up. That's when they brought him to Weredale House.

The tall one is Gary. The shorter one is Bryan. Gary says I smoke funny. Sometimes when I'm practicing in the bathroom I don't choke or cough, my eyes just water a little. I'm getting better. But when I'm standing behind the school with the Weredale boys I always end up choking and coughing so bad, they both laugh at me.

"You have to hold it in," Gary says, "like this." Then he slowly inhales, without coughing or choking. Show off.

"You should smoke Export A," says Gary. He takes half the cigarettes from my pack. "You can afford it," he says, handing me the now half-empty pack.

We meet at the back of the school every day during lunchtime. They never eat anything either.

"The food at Weredale is just shit," says Gary as he tosses his paper bag in the garbage each day.

I wish I could know what's in that bag. It looks pretty full. I don't know what Bryan does with his lunch. Maybe he eats it when he's alone so he won't have to share. He makes me bring him ten cents to school every day now. If I don't bring the ten cents I think they'll stop talking to me and maybe even beat me up. I'm not afraid of them. They aren't pigs at all and they never act icky or creepy with me. But I'm afraid they'll stop talking to me. Somehow I've become invisible to everyone else. Gary and Bryan are the only people who act like I exist. Sometimes other people will pretend to see me but I can tell they're faking. Mr. Levy asks me if there are any girls in the class that I'm friends with.

"You don't have to hang around with Gary and Bryan all the time," he says. "I bet lots of other students in the class would be happy to be your friend. Would you like me to talk to anyone? Maybe one of the girls? Are any of the girls friends with you?"

If I had a gun I might have shot him.

"Please don't talk to anyone," I say. "The other girls all like me but I try to be friends with everyone. I don't think it's right not to talk to somebody just because they don't live in a nice home and have parents and stuff like most of these kids do, right?"

I'm relieved when it works.

"Oh no, no, no!" says Mr. Levy. "I think it's great that you're friends with the two boys from Weredale of course! I just thought maybe you could also…well, no, it's just great." Then he smiles at me and I know I'm dismissed.

Mom gave me a small book that closes with a zipper for my twelfth birthday.

"You keep saying you want to be a writer," says Mom. "So write. It's where you can keep all your secrets."

She points at the small zipper.

"You can keep them all under lock and key."

There's no lock. Or key. Just a zipper. The diary is a small light blue square. The pages are lined and numbered. I want to say that Beth's the real writer. She's the only one in the family who not only wrote a letter to the Prime Minister of Canada, but even got a reply. Mr. Trudeau told Beth that his secretary, whose name is also Beth, had thought her letter was so delightful, she brought it to his attention. Even Dad was super impressed by Beth practically being a pen pal of the fucking Prime Minister of fucking Canada.

"Be nice if your new pal could get me a house like the one for sale on Wellington Street," said Mom. The house has seven bedrooms and not one but two bathrooms. Mom actually went and looked at it but they want $45,000 for it.

"Might as well be a million," said Mom.

Beth wrote a second letter to her new rich friend, asking him if he'd consider lending our mom $45,000.

"I know she'd pay you back," wrote Beth. "My mother is a very honest and hard working person."

She never heard from Mr. Trudeau again. The fucker.

My sisters know about my diary and they keep looking for it, but they'll never find it. Mom did though. She left a note on one of the pages about me smoking.

"Where are you getting those cigarettes?" says Mom's message in my diary.

She knows they're not coming from her pack. Usually I smoke Menthols, which Mom calls mint flavoured shit sticks.

"The only things that should be mint-flavoured are gum and mouth wash. Cigarettes are supposed to taste like cigarettes," she says.

I don't really like Menthols that much either, but most of the time they're the only cigarettes I can get my hands on. They're the only ones on display right out on the counter. They're attached to a large cardboard sign that says, "Smoke Menthols for that cool refreshing taste!"

I've started a second diary and now the blue one with the zipper is just a decoy. I have to remember to write stuff in it every once in a while, just to throw Mom off track.

"Dear Diary, I'm so lucky. I have a wonderful family. We all love each other so much."

Mom can bite me. I wouldn't be surprised to walk into the kitchen one day and hear her reading it out loud to her gang. In my real diary, I keep a list of everything I steal each week from Duffy's Variety and the store near my school.

"How much money did you bring me?" Gary asks like he does every day.

He doesn't know I live in the Point. I feel proud that him and Bryan actually think I'm one of the dumbass rich kids from Westmount, able to give them a dime every single day. But it's getting harder to find the money. I skipped school three times this month when I knew I wouldn't be able to make the payment.

"I don't have anything today," I say then try to change the subject.

"Wanna go rip something off at the Indian store?"

There's a small store stuffed with all kinds of shit at the corner near the school. The place is run by a bunch of real Indians from India, not the Caughnawaga kind. There are rows and rows of all kinds of strange things. Small metal bowls with lids, nice smelling sticks, tiny half naked fat guys made of brass, weird looking food. And at the cash they have menthol cigarettes. Never my first choice but not bad for free.

"I want my dime," says Bryan. "Where's our money?"

When I say I couldn't get it today they both give me a hard look.

"You aren't really our friend, are you?" says Gary. "You're just one of them posers, a fake. You're just too good for us."

I start to say they're wrong but they both ignore me and start to walk away. I run behind them, trying to catch up.

"No, really, wait! Guys, hang on! I'm sorry. I promise I'll have it tomorrow. Seriously, I will! Want a Black Cat cigarette?"

The Black Cat cigarettes get them. Aunt Olive gave me half a pack. She lifted them from Duffy's Variety yesterday but she thinks they taste like shitty tires. She smoked fourteen of them before she decided they'd give her fucking lung cancer if she didn't stop, so I only got ten. I have six left to share though and I know Gary and Bryan will think the package is cool.

"Look, it's a Black Cat on the front for real!"

Gary rips the package out of my hand and has a closer look at the cat.

"Fucking lame," he says. "Those are girl's smokes," and he drops the package onto the ground.

"You don't have to be an asshole about it!" I say then bend over to pick them up.

I sensed the foot before I actually felt it. A second later I was doing a face plant and listening to Bryan's annoying high-pitched laughter.

"Don't you call me an asshole!" says Gary. He's standing over me.

I keep an eye on him while I jump to my feet.

"Fuck you!" I scream an inch from his face.

The punch to my chin knocks me flat again and for a second I feel stunned. I shake my head like they do sometimes in a cartoon and I'm amazed to realize those spinning stars aren't just fake for TV. Before I can shake all the stars away, Gary has yanked me to my feet. I can feel my shirt ripping. I see his fist coming at my face again and just before I close my eyes, I see him suddenly yanked backward. Like a silent bomb has gone off and blown him away from me. Mr. Levy is holding Gary up in the air by the back of his neck with one hand.

"What's going on here?" asks Mr. Levy. He's looking at me. Gary's neck is still in his hand. His feet aren't touching the ground.

"Somebody better start talking real soon!"

Gary suddenly breaks free of Mr. Levy's grip and is spinning around towards him. Suddenly he's flat on his back and Mr. Levy has a foot on his chest.

"Don't even think about it buddy. Don't even think about it!"

Bryan has his arms folded across his chest and is glaring at me, nodding his head.

"We were just fooling around!" I say, leaning down to pull on Mr. Levy's foot. "Seriously, we were just kidding around."

Mr. Levy takes a step back and Gary is on his feet instantly. He doesn't look at me or Mr. Levy.

"I want all three of you in my classroom, NOW," says Mr. Levy. Then he turns and walks away. We follow behind him without saying a word. I sneak a look at Gary but he's ignoring me. I look at Bryan and he gives me the finger. I give it back.

"Mr. Levy is a lot faster than he looks," I say to my sisters on the bus ride home. "He had that kid up so fast I thought a giant hook had grabbed him!"

Annie is looking at the red spot on my chin and I can tell she's doing one of her slow burns.

"Where did you say these two fuckers live?"

I know she's already plotting.

"It's nothing," I say. "Really, it's okay. They're my friends. We were just fooling around and Mr. Levy didn't understand what was going on. He must have thought they were hurting me. After we got to class he went and got me some ice from the office and held it on my chin himself!"

Annie and Ruth grin at each other. Fuck.

"Somebody's in looooove," they chant together. "Kathy loooooooves Mr. Levy. L-O-V-E-S..."

Bitches.

"You shut the fuck up right now or I swear to God I'll toss your books out the bus window!"

Annie stops laughing and holds onto her books tighter.

"You need to tell Mom what's going on," says Ruth.

Later that night, Mom yells for me to come to the kitchen.

"What happened at school today with those two boys?"

Shit.

"It was no big deal. I promised to loan one of them ten cents and..."

Mom interrupts me. "Are those two little fuckers from Weredale shaking you down? Are they? The goddamn nerve of the little shits."

It's been a while since I've seen Mom so angry.

"I'm going with you to the school tomorrow!"

I must have spent the next two hours going back and forth from the living room to the kitchen, to Mom's bedroom, just following her around and begging her not to go to school with me.

"If you do that you might as well pull me out now because then I'll be invisible full-time, even during recess and lunch, every single day!"

I tell her how they're the only two in the whole school besides me who don't know their timetables or the names of each province, and they don't think that means a person is stupid. They don't care about me not knowing anything.

"They say it just means you hate school more than the keeners!"

Mom finally caves and promises not to go to the school with me. I make her swear on her life and then I'm finally able to go to bed. Just before I fall asleep, I suddenly remember. I still need a fucking dime. Two nickels. Ten cents. Fuck.

The next morning I keep trying to catch Bryan and Gary's eye but they both ignore me. When the bell goes for recess, Mr. Levy stands in front of me and says I need to stay in the classroom.

"I need to speak with you," he says.

His voice makes me feel all nervous inside. It's like he's mad at me. I try to remember if I've done anything he might have found out about but the only thing I can think of is the shit he already knows about. Maybe the boys told him I owe them some money and aren't paying them back? I was forty cents behind now.

"I spoke with the principal this morning right after I got in," says Mr. Levy. "He wanted to speak with me because of a call he got from your mother."

Fuck. Me.

"Apparently Gary and Bryan have been using intimidation tactics to force you to steal money to pay them some kind of a shakedown fee each day. Is that true?"

I hate my mother.

"And apparently they've somehow managed to isolate you and make you feel like the rest of your classmates don't wish to associate with you?"

Mr. Levy hates me. Please god, let me be dead.

"I thought we had resolved the issue yesterday ourselves right here in the classroom. Please tell me if I'm wrong, but if I recall correctly, you sat right in that chair and told me to my face, insisted to my face, that you three are close friends and I had misunderstood what my own eyes were telling me. As a teacher, I fully understand and appreciate the crucial importance of allowing students the opportunity to resolve their own issues and find solutions to their own conflicts. Now I realize I should have trusted my instincts and…"

Mr. Levy kneels down next to me. I angrily wipe the tears away. God, I hate myself.

"Kathy, why didn't you come to me? Why didn't you ask for my help?"

You mean, why did I keep you out of the loop, allowing my mom to go over your head and make you look like a clueless wonder who doesn't know what the hell is going on in his own class?

"I'm sorry," I say. "I'm sorry. My mom swore she wasn't going to do anything, she swore she understood what I meant. She just didn't want to lend me the ten cents."

Mr. Levy stands up.

"We're going to have another meeting, the three of us," he says and then holds up a hand when I try to interrupt. "This problem gets fixed today. Right now. It's over."

Mr. Levy sends me into the hallway. Gary and Bryan are both sitting there. He waves them into the room. They won't look at me as they get up from the bench. I sit down. My life is over. I'm never going to talk to my mother again. Ever. Why does she want to ruin my life? She's just evil.

It seems to take forever before Mr. Levy opens the classroom door again. I had tried listening but couldn't hear anything at all.

"Come on in," says Mr. Levy.

When I walk into the class both of the boys look up at me. I try to read their faces but can't tell what they're thinking.

"We're really sorry," says Gary. "We shouldn't have asked you to…" he looks at Mr. Levy for a minute, "…lend us anything."

"We didn't know you're from the Point!" says Bryan. "I swear I ain't like that!"

"I thought you lived around here, maybe in the apartment buildings across from the Indian store, sure, but…"

Mr. Levy interrupts. "You understand what you were doing is inappropriate with any student, regardless…"

"Sure, sure," says Gary, "Of course. We got it." Then he looks down.

Mr. Levy makes some more speeches about the power of friendship and the support you can only get if you blah, blah, blah, and some other shit. I tune him out. I'm wondering if my face is on fire and if any of them can tell just by looking at me.

"Can I go now?" I ask. Then the bell rings and we all know the rest of the class will be outside the door in a couple of minutes. Mr. Levy stands up.

"We'll see how this progresses in the future, but I think we might have all learned something important here today."

Yeah, that I hate my mother. I hate Gary and Bryan. And I hate you, Mr. Levy.

Later in the yard during lunch break, Gary and Bryan both approach me.

"Mr. Levy is right," says Gary. "You are the last person we should have asked for, you know, like anything."

Bryan pulls out his pack of Export A. "Here, take them. Really. Go ahead."

They feel sorry for me? They fucking feel sorry for me?

"Why don't you just go fuck yourself," I say to Bryan, "Just fuck off."

The look on both of their faces almost makes me laugh out loud.

"You fucking cunt," says Bryan. "You cheap piece of Point St. Charles fucking ass. Who the fuck do you think…"

They don't follow me when I walk away. I can hear Bryan's

"cheap bitch" and "whore" echoing in my head for the rest of the day. On the way home, I lean my head against the bus window. Even Ruth and Annie don't seem to see me.

I write in my diary when I get home. The decoy one, the one I want to make sure she'd see. Bitch.

"I hate my mother. She's evil and hates me even more than I hate her. She's ruined my life. Everyone who knows me that matters now hates my guts. Mr. Levy is a jerk. I hope he falls off a cliff. I hope he gets hit by a truck. I hope he eats shit and dies. Why is everybody such a fucking liar?"

The next day at school, I pretend to listen as Mr. Levy talks about the British Influence on Canada's parliament and other boring shit. Why did I ever think this guy was interesting? I thought I'd be happy forever, just listening to his voice while doing attendance. I used to like how after he says your name, he looks up and then smiles after you say, "Here." I think about how it used to annoy the shit out of me when he smiles at Jessica Murray after she says, "Here," or anybody else in the classroom. I think about his hand when he held the ice to my chin. It seems like all that had happened a billion years ago.

After holding the cold baggie against my chin for a few minutes, he took my hand and placed it over the ice, showing me where to hold it.

"Just keep it right here, okay?" then he smiled at me. Why did it make my stomach ache when he smiled at me? When I found out Mr. Levy has kids I was shocked. I had thought he liked other kids so much because he didn't have any of his own. Maybe his kids are idiots or something? Mom said one time that teachers' children are often the biggest jerks in the school.

"It's often easier to know what to do when they aren't your own," said Mom.

Mr. Levy is still being all boring. I raise my hand to go to the washroom and after I get the nod I leave the classroom. Once safely inside one of the stalls, suddenly I can't stop crying. I don't know what the hell is wrong with me. I'm such a freak. Just a fucking freak. I'm afraid someone is going to hear me but if I leave the stall someone might walk in and see me. I wish I could quit school and get a job. My cousin Meghan says Bell is hiring. I'd have to fake that I know more French than I actually do but Meghan says they need workers so maybe I'd be able to pull it off. It's not like I'd be an operator or anything, so how much French would I really need? I wonder how old you have to be before they'll give you a full-time job?

When some kids come into the washroom, I open the door to the stall and leave.

Chapter Eight

IT'S EASY TO SPOT A BAILIFF when they come to your door. They try to dress up like they're from the Point, wearing stuff like a leather vest and black jeans as if that makes them look tough. Nobody in the Point dresses like that. I don't know anyone in the Point who thinks their clothing can make them look tough. They just wear whatever they can get their hands on.

One time I accidentally opened the door when a bailiff knocked. Usually we all go quiet and stop moving when somebody knocks, but I forgot to check before opening the door. I instantly realized my mistake when I saw the vest and dark jeans standing in front of me.

"Are your parents home?" the bailiff asked.

He had a ponytail, which I guess was part of his tough guy outfit. I wanted to tell him that guys with ponytails get the shit kicked out of them faster than a Pepper can say *tabernac*.

I didn't say anything for a couple seconds. Should I slam the door shut in his face?

"*Parlez-vous français?*" Maybe if I pretended to speak French he'd just go away. Please don't let him say '*Oui*.'

"Are your parents home?" the bailiff repeated, saying each word slowly. Maybe he could see right through my horrible French accent?

"*Mange de la marde!*" I quickly shut the door. He pounded for a few seconds, mad as hell at the sound of my sisters and I all laughing, I guess. We shouted, "Fuck off!" and "I don't speak the good English!" We would have played with him for as long as he stood there, banging on the door, calling us little cunts and stupid bitches before finally storming away.

"You Point St. Charles pieces of shit!" he yelled as he got back into his car.

"You fucking loser!" I yelled back through the mailbox. "Why don't you get a real job!"

Dad still keeps trying to get Mom to agree to move out of the Point. I bet he'd live with us every day if we did and then they could stop fighting about it all the time, too.

"Don't you want more for our girls?" says Dad. "Do you want them to grow up here, surrounded by all of this filth? Do you want them to marry a boy from the Point and get stuck here forever?"

"There's nothing wrong with Point St. Charles!" says Mom. "Who the hell are you anyway to turn your nose up at the Point? That's your mother talking!"

Dad never likes it when Mom brings his mother into their fights.

"There's no need to slander my mother," says Dad quietly. "But maybe if you had even just a touch of her class you'd..."

"I'd fucking what? Despise my own children? Turn my nose up at my friends? Think I'm better than anybody else just because I'm a good fucking Christian woman? Don't make me choose, Russ."

"Why is it hypocritical of you to live somewhere else?" asks Dad. "What's wrong with wanting to live somewhere clean and safe and with decent people? How does that make you part of the Establishment?"

"The Point is a real community," says Mom, "and unless we all join the fight and support each other we'll never be able to..."

"You sound like a parrot," says Dad. "That's just your commie friends from the clinic talking. It's me you're talking to, Eileen. Me."

After Dad left, Mom got all quiet for a while. She sat at the kitchen table reading the newspaper with a large bag of plain Humpty Dumpty chips ripped open on the table in front of her. We knew not to ask for any.

The next morning when I got up Dad was back and was piling a bunch of stuff near the door. He had a pile of hangers with his dress shirts draped over his arm.

"You know I can't live like this," he says to Mom.

I'm not sure if she heard him. She's just sitting at the kitchen table staring at her coffee mug, smoking a Player's. Dad looks at her for a minute, then turns back to the pile of stuff at the door. I want to beg him to stay, to swear I'll keep the place clean. But I know he won't believe me. My sisters and I are always swearing things are going to be different, that we'll take turns sweeping the floor and cleaning the dishes. I wish we weren't such pigs, but we can't help ourselves. I thought everything would change once Mom got her full-time job with the clinic. That her and Dad wouldn't fight anymore since Mom wouldn't be yelling at him about what he spends his money on instead of spending it on us. Some things did change. Like we nearly always have something for supper and Mom buys stuff like shampoo now and even Kotex for when we're bleeding. I'm so happy not to have to wear the same pad for my whole period anymore. Mom usually gets enough that I can change it once a day, rewrapping it at school with some fresh toilet paper from the bathroom.

I thought our days of pulling a midnight move were over but a couple of days after Dad left with all of his nice shirts and the hangers they were on, Mom found us a place back on Bourgeoys Street again, but this one is closer to the train tracks. I claim the upstairs landing as soon as I spot it. There's just enough room to shove a single bed under the window. It feels a little weird at first not sleeping in a bunk bed with a sister up above or below, but I like that I can stare out the window at night and see the Redpath Sugar factory sign glowing red. It makes a perfect nightlight.

"I dare you to run by the trains naked," I say to Annie one night. Mom is working late at one of her meetings and it's raining a little.

"Only if we all do it," she says.

Thirty seconds later, after three chicken out, three of us dash into the yard when we hear the train coming, waving frantically to the passengers as it whizzes by.

"Look at them gawking at our naked slave girl titties!" we shriek, laughing and shaking our arms so hard, we have to hold on to each other as the train passes. When I see their shocked faces pressed up against the windows, I know I'm not invisible.

The next time we pull a midnight move it isn't because the

landlord is asking for his rent.

"We're taking a vacation from your father," Mom explains as she stuffs a couple of blankets into a garbage bag.

We move into the apartment on Wellington Street, the one where her commie friends have knocked a hole into the wall. Dad says the commies never have TVs because that would make them part of the Establishment, but there's a big record player in the corner.

"Can I play a record?" I ask Seth, not really expecting him to say yes. It's practically the size of a table and says "Ultra Stereogram" in big letters across the front. It looks expensive.

"Yes, of course. Anything inside this apartment that's ours is yours, too," he says, smiling.

I think he said yes because he didn't know he was allowed to say no. He's sitting at the table talking to my mom, but I don't think he can really hear what she's saying. He keeps looking over at the record player, swinging his head back and forth between my mom and us.

"You guys alright? Do you know how to put the records in? Need any help?" he finally asks.

Me, Annie, and Ruth are still trying to decide which one to listen to. There are so many records on the shelves it looks like a library, except with The Beatles, Janice Joplin, and Cat Stevens instead of books. Even with all the good music sitting right in front of us, Ruth manages to find Itsy Bitsy Teenie Weenie Yellow Polka Dot Bikini.

"There's no way we're listening to that one," I say, looking through the shelves.

"Well, you've been very quiet," Seth says, looking at Julia. Me and Annie and Ruth are looking through the records but Julia is just standing behind us, quiet like she always is.

"Which songs do you like to listen to?" Seth asks her, smiling. "What kind of music do you enjoy?"

Seth keeps talking to Julia for a couple minutes, asking her stuff like what her favourite songs are, and then he tells her she can pick which record to listen to first. Julia looks through the shelves, and then silently pulls out a Bob Dylan record. I want to tell Seth that she doesn't even know what she's doing, that she probably just likes the cover of the record, with the man and woman walking down the street together. But he smiles and drops the record onto the player, then goes back to the table with my mom.

I remind myself that I need to be more quiet sometimes. Dad says I talk too much, and I never understood what he meant. How can someone talk too much? But I think I get it now. If you're all quiet and shy, grown-ups try to draw stuff out of you.

I'm glad when we move back to the apartment on Bourgeoys Street—the one where I can see the Redpath Sugar factory sign at night, because for the first time ever, I have my own room.

"It's not a real bedroom," Ruth says after Mom agrees I can use the upstairs landing for my room.

"Says who?" I ask.

"There's a staircase right there," Ruth points out triumphantly, like a staircase being nearby means I'm not allowed to call it a bedroom. Everyone has to walk through the upstairs landing to get to the other rooms, but I don't care. I think Ruth's just jealous because she didn't think of it first.

Julia is crying and lying down in front of the oil stove again. Mom doesn't have a quarter to fill it with oil but Julia is still lying down in the hallway, saying her stomach hurts and rubbing it until she falls asleep. Mom's been bringing her to doctors but they say it's all in Julia's head. The other day Mom took a screaming fit in the ER at the Children's. Belinda Mavory had told her she needs to make sure they hear her concerns. Mom takes Belinda's advice.

"I'm not leaving this fucking waiting room until the fucking chief of staff comes down here and checks my child's goddamn appendix before the fucking thing BURSTS!" she shouts. "And if it does I swear to god I'll be kicking your royal asses all over this damn city!"

I'm not sure if it was the chief of staff who checked Julia's appendix, but they poked and prodded and X-rayed poor Julia who has been getting skinnier and quieter for the past few months now.

"Don't be sleeping in front of the heater," Mom tells Julia when they get home from the ER.

Julia waits until Mom is asleep before sneaking into the hallway and curling up in front of the heater like a cat. I think Mom's worried that the heater might blow up with Julia curled up right in front of it. Heaters like that are always catching fire in the Point. Sometimes they blow up because of the oil. When we woke up one time and the apartment was on fire I was afraid that Julia had blown up, but the fire wasn't in the hallway. It was in the bedroom, under one of the beds.

"Get the hell out!" Mom yelled at us, filling a pot up at the tub and running back into the bedroom.

I was glad Dad was home that night. If he hadn't been there to help Mom put the fire out, she would have had to call the fire department.

"Must have been some wires in the walls," Dad said to Mom once the fire was put out. "They got too hot, I guess."

To be honest, I think it was all the junk we had shoved under the bed that caught fire.

"If you girls ever stay inside again while the house or apartment is burning I'll be very angry and disappointed with you," said Dad in a quiet voice.

We had all been trying to carry stuff out of the apartment in case Mom and Dad couldn't put it out. We couldn't just leave and watch the house burn down from outside while Mom and Dad were still inside.

"Your homework is important, Annie," Mom said, "but if you ever go running back for it when we tell you to get out, I'll kick your ass. And if you have to grab something, maybe you should save some of your clothes or some blankets next time, eh?"

We were all up late that night, trying to wave the bad smell out the windows and put away the mountain of stuff Ruth and Annie had piled up near the door. We would've hauled it out to the curb if Dad hadn't got the fire out soon enough.

A few days after Julia's visit to the ER with Mom, the hospital calls and says they want Julia back in as soon as possible. I think the doctors have finally figured out what's wrong with her. I was secretly worried she was turning into a zombie since she never talks anymore and is so skinny and white, you can see right through her.

The doctors must have felt bad about not figuring it out faster because she ended up having an operation to fix what was wrong with her two days later. Dad doesn't think it was because of the doctors feeling bad though.

"I'm glad your hippie friends came through and were useful for once," he says.

When Mom just looks at him, Dad tries to explain. "You know, they pulled some strings and instead of her being stuck on some waiting list for half a year, they compromised their commie principles and for once did what was in the best interest of the 'few'."

Mom says Julia made medical history for being the youngest person in Canada to ever be operated on for gallstones.

"It's not usually something a child that young gets," says Mom.

Dad says Julia has a million-dollar view in her room. At night you can look out the window and see the whole city at once. One whole wall of her room is made of glass and if you look out when it's dark enough, you can see the lights of the Point and the cross on Mount Royal at the same time. Julia has tons and tons of visitors and half of them bring her stuff, too. Stuffed cats, dogs, a real Barbie doll with tiny black shoes, a deck of playing cards, some hand cream and even some 'Get Well Soon' cards with money inside of them. Three times a day the nurses bring her a tray filled with all kinds of food. Toast with peanut butter, eggs, a tiny box with Corn Flakes in it, a small container of milk, and a glass of juice. That's just for breakfast.

"They're trying to make me fat," says Julia with a small grin. She's looking better already. Beside her bed she has a pill container filled with tiny rocks.

"This is what they took out of me," she says, holding it up to the light. "I had over a hundred of them in my gallbladder!"

I would kill myself before asking Julia where in hell a gall-bladder is, or what exactly it does, other than filling up with rocks and making you lay down in front of an oil heater. If she knows what a gallbladder is then I should too, her being younger than me and all.

"Can I look at those rocks?" I ask. They're all kinds of colours and different sizes, too.

"Sure. Do you want some of those?" Julia asks, pointing at the collection of tiny cereal boxes on the side table next to her bed. A chair nearby holds all of her new stuffed toys and dolls and the Barbie with the perfect little shoes. On the window ledge is a pair of binoculars. I've never seen them up close before.

"Can I look in those?" I ask. I hold them up to my eyes and try to see my night light, the Redpath Sugar sign, through the window. I can't find it. But I find the cross on Mount Royal.

"Doesn't it look cool?" says Julia.

It seems like Julia is in the hospital for a long time. She's so lucky. When she finally comes back home again she's like a different person. The nurses had washed and braided her long thin hair almost every day.

"Daddy came and saw me every single day at the hospital and rubbed cream onto my hands," says Julia. "The nurses all kept telling me what a handsome man my father is and how funny he is, too."

Julia had the rest of the bottle hidden away until it was all gone. Like I'd want any of that stuff on my hands anyway. She shared everything else though: the food, the toys, even the money. From then on, after coming home from the hospital, Julia tries to wash her hair all the time and keep her hands clean and soft. If she has clean socks, she wears them to bed. Sometimes she lets us look at her scar and container of tiny rocks. She never sleeps in front of the hallway heater again.

Next week we're all starting back at school, even Julia since her scar is finally all closed up and dry now. One time it leaked everywhere, scaring the shit out of Mom. It was the middle of the night and Julia woke up and gave Mom a little shake, saying she needed to wake up. When Mom saw the blood all over the sheets she screamed like she had found Julia with a knife sticking out of her. It was Belinda Mavory who came over with her car and drove Julia and Mom to the ER. Belinda never even said one word about the mess in her car. After Julia came back from the hospital her scar finally stayed dry and closed up for good.

Next week I start grade seven at Westmount High and Mom says she might be able to get me some jeans eventually, maybe even by Christmas. Until then, I'm going to have to wear the pair of brown pants she got me from St. Columba House.

"They fit you perfectly!" she says after I pull them on and come out of my room to show her.

"Yeah but they aren't jeans," I say.

"I know, I know," Mom says impatiently, "I already told you, I'll get you some jeans as soon as I can afford to."

Mom doesn't get how important it is for me to look right. At this school I have another shot. I get to start all over again. Except for the jeans, I almost feel ready for Westmount High. I even have a real purse I can bring thanks to Nanny.

"Here dear, this is for you," says Nanny, handing me a package wrapped in brown paper.

I open up the crinkled paper and inside is one of her old church purses. The small square one made of pink vinyl with a white plastic daisy attached to the front, with a small snap that opens up the purse. I've always loved that purse. It's perfect.

"Wow, I don't even know what to say, Nanny!"

"You don't have to say anything. I was going to put it in my box for the church anyway and then I thought maybe you could use it for that new fancy high school you'll be starting at next week."

I wrap my arms around Nanny and hug her close.

"You stop that now," she laughs, swatting me away, "I can't even breathe!"

I pull on the daisy to open the purse and find a crisp dollar bill inside.

"Nanny, you forgot this!" I say, holding out the dollar.

"Don't be silly, you goose," says Nanny. "That's for you."

I feel my face blushing a bit as I walk home from Nanny's with the purse hanging off my shoulder like it's always been there. I can see kids staring as I walk by. When I get home I take it off before one of the girls see it. Now all I need is the right clothes. Mom swears she'll get me some jeans as soon as she can but until then I'll have to wear my brown slacks since they're the only ones I have. They might be a little too fancy, though. They have cuffs at the bottom and I think that means a rich person used to wear them until they donated them to St. Columba House. I'm going to feel like an asshole walking to the bus stop wearing them. I know that if I saw a kid in the Point wearing them I'd probably want to beat them up, too. But it's only a quick walk to the bus and once I sit down, nobody will really see them anyway.

The next week I avoid eye contact with everyone as I walk to the bus stop, even the stupid Pepper who tries to start something by stepping out in front of me on purpose. Like I couldn't beat the living shit out of her just because I'm all dressed up. At the last second I look up and make a mental note of what she looks like. Later, bitch. I'll remember you for later.

The first morning at Westmount High goes by pretty fast. At first I'm really nervous, worried I'll get lost or be late for a class, but I finally do what Mom told me to do and look for a friendly face to ask for help. Some girls who look around my age are standing by their lockers, smiling and laughing with each other. They look nice.

"Excuse me," I say, with what feels like a big fake grin. "Can one of you help me, please? I'm trying to find room 2107B."

They all stop talking and stare.

"That's on the second floor," says one of them with a smile. "The 'B' means it's on the left side."

"Where'd you get the purse?" asks another girl. "Your grandmother?" All of her friends laugh.

I turn and walk the other way. How the hell did they know I got the purse from my grandmother? I turn around a corner and take the stairs to the next floor. I quickly yank off the purse and stuff it into the large garbage can outside a classroom. It isn't until later that I remember the dollar bill inside.

"Welcome to grade seven science class," says the teacher standing at the front of the room. "My name is Mrs. Schwartz and

I will be expecting a lot from you this year."

Although she's speaking to the entire class I feel like she's just looking at me the whole time.

"This year we'll look at the States of Matter, Concepts of Temperature, and Interactions within Ecosystems, among other related subjects and issues."

The girl sitting next to me is scribbling into a notebook. Every time the teacher utters a word, the girl writes in her notebook. I look around and realize everybody is writing.

Next is English class.

"I want to learn what each and every one of you think," says the teacher. "I'm going to give you ample opportunities to share your insights and ideas on a whole range of themes and topics that we'll delve more into next week."

Then she hands out what she calls the Reading List and tells us we can either buy the books ourselves or borrow them from the library. I scan the list and I'm surprised to see I've actually already read a few. *David Copperfield* and *The Catcher in the Rye* are two of the books I got from the People's Library in the Point when Ruth was working there. I've already read *Of Mice and Men*, too, after Annie said it was her favourite book in the whole wide world. Maybe I read the book too fast but I never did see any mice in that story. A few others on the list look interesting, too. *The Adventures of Huckleberry Finn*, and *Are You There, God? It's Me, Margaret*. Nanny would be glad to know I'm reading something with God in it.

I thought geography class would be all about the parts of the world I know I'm never going to see, so at first I'm excited. But it turns out to be a whole lot less interesting than I hoped. The teacher asks me to show him where Peru is on a big map hanging in the front of the class. I walk up to the map and try to find it but there are too many little names written everywhere. Egypt, North Africa, Chad. Where the fuck is Peru?

"Uhhh, ummm," I say, as if I'm on the brink of finding Peru.

Maybe I could find it on the map if I was on a deserted island for ten years. And Annie was with me. But I'm standing in front of the whole class and the teacher is right beside me. I can see him frowning out of the corner of my eye. He finally tells me to sit down and asks someone else where Peru is. The boy walks up to the map and points right away.

"Peru is in western South America."

Fucking show off. The teacher looks relieved, like he had been worried that he got a dumb class.

"Which country borders Peru… to the North?" the teacher asks. He points to a girl sitting at the front of the class.

"Ecuador and Colombia," she answers.

I guess all my classes can't be winners.

I haven't said a word yet in any of the classes. I just sit there listening and watching, like I might somehow become part of the class if I keep still long enough. But when I find a desk and sit down in home economics, the girl sitting behind me starts being friendly.

"I'm Karen!" she says with a smile.

She talks at me for a few minutes but before I can answer the teacher is telling the class to settle down. Home economics isn't at all what I expected. Apparently we're going to learn how to make aprons, cookies, and a stuffed toy. I've never seen Mom wearing an apron. I thought only people in cartoons wore them. When the bell goes the teacher asks me to stay behind. I immediately wonder what I've done wrong. No one has seemed to notice me yet except for that one girl, Karen, who went out of her way to be all nice and friendly. I'd been worrying that I was going to be invisible again but Karen seems like she might become a friend. Maybe a good friend. Once the classroom empties out the teacher looks over and waves me to her desk.

"Welcome to Westmount High. I know you're part of a special integration program this year so I wanted to mention something to you, privately of course, away from prying ears," she says. "We do have a…um, a special fund for… special circumstances. You know," she continues, nodding her head at me like I should know how to finish her sentence. I have no clue what she's trying to say though.

"That three dollar fee I mentioned in class earlier? And the twenty-two dollars for later? Don't you worry a thing about that, okay? We'll take care of it. Just tell your mother to give me a call and…"

Three dollar fee? Twenty-two fucking dollars? When in hell did she mention that? In class? While I was there? All I can remember is her talking about fucking aprons, stuffed shit, and cookies. What's this about twenty-two dollars?

"And we'll make sure no one even knows, right? Okay?" the teacher is smiling at me. I know she's expecting something.

"Uh, well, thanks, I guess."

I don't think that's the answer she wanted or expected. Her face seems to harden and she suddenly stands up.

"You better get going or you'll be late for your next class."

My next class is math. The teacher freaks me out a bit. She's super tall for a woman and has a big limp. One leg is shorter than the other but the whole class seems unaware of her limp as she hobbles around the classroom, talking so fast I barely understand a word she's saying. Mind you, it being math and all, she could speak as slowly as my Aunt Rachel after her stroke last year and I still wouldn't know what the hell she's talking about. When she hands out the textbooks I know I'm doomed just from the cover. It has a picture of the times tables right on the front. When the bell finally rings I can't wait to get out of that classroom. I'm dying to go pee. A few minutes later I'm finally sitting down and have just finished wiping myself with a huge wad of free toilet paper when I hear them. I wasn't listening at first, I was too busy making a pencil roll of toilet paper to take home. Then my brain registers the words "new girl" and I tune in.

"And what about those pathetic pants? Do you think she borrowed them off an uncle?"

Once they finish laughing and are calm enough to speak again, one of them says, "Or maybe stole them off a dead body?"

They laugh so hard at that I'm sure a teacher passing by will stick their head in to check things out. I slowly lift up my feet and hold them flat against the door. Please, please don't let them find me.

"She's such a loser," says Karen. I recognize her voice. "I think she's even retarded. My mom said they were going to let a whole bunch of retards come here as part of some pilot study."

I feel sick. I'm so stupid. I had really thought Karen liked me. Had even liked my pants.

"OMIGOD, I LOVE those pants!" she had said to me earlier, just minutes before home economics class had started.

"Look at these!" she had said to the girls standing behind me, showing off my pants so proudly you would have thought they were her own.

"Have you ever seen anything like these before? They even have cuffs!"

Then she winked at me. I thought the wink meant we were going to be friends.

"She has two older sisters here, too," says another voice in the bathroom. "Did you hear what happened when Mr. Thomas asked Deb to be nice to the older one their first year here? She invited her over to her house for lunch and, get this, she actually asked if she could bring her other sister with her!"

The other girls giggle.

"Then didn't the two of them eat like they hadn't eaten a thing in days! Deb says her mother told her to leave the husky horses at school from then on!"

Suddenly a teacher is talking. "Come on girls, time to break up the party. The bell is going to ring in a minute. Let's go!"

I wait a few more minutes before lowering my feet. I peek out into the hallway before leaving the bathroom, making sure it's clear. The bell rings and a few minutes later I'm seated in English class pretending not to notice Karen and her friends all sitting nearby. Just before the teacher walks in, Karen suddenly yells over, "Hey, new girl!" and when I look up, she stage whispers, "Love the pants!" Then gives me a huge grin.

When I see Ruth and Annie on the bus, they ask how my first day was. I don't tell them about Karen or what the other girls in the bathroom said.

"It was alright," I say.

I wonder if the same thing happened to Ruth and Annie on their first day. They probably wouldn't have said anything about Annie's clothes, though. She always wears really nice dresses and curls her hair every night before going to sleep. Out of the three of us, Annie looks the most like a rich girl.

If Ruth and Annie hadn't been on the bus with me I might have missed our stop. I was staring out the window and thinking about those girls in the bathroom again, wondering how different things would have been if I had been wearing jeans.

"Kathy, come on," Annie says when we get to our stop.

When I get home I go into the bathroom. I had seen someone in math class looking at my hands and when I looked down at them I saw there was dirt around my nails. Now standing in the bathroom at home, I try rubbing the dirt out but it seems stuck there. I look in the mirror and see dirt on my elbows, too. It's the first time I've ever really noticed it. No matter how much I scrub at the dirt, it doesn't want to come out. I have Point St. Charles elbows and hands. So dirty they'll never get clean.

The next day in English class Mrs. Enrich says we're going to write an argumentative essay.

"Which means you will take a position on an issue- one very important to all of us here I'm sure—to defend and argue. With both sides of an issue explored, you learn more about it."

I didn't know you could argue in a classroom with a teacher around. This was sounding interesting for sure.

"As we all know," says Mrs. Enrich, "an issue very near and dear to our hearts is that some real estate developers are considering buying land in Westmount Park. Now let's have a little thought experiment. What would be some of the problems with that?" she asks.

So much for exploring both sides of the issue.

"All the squirrels and other wildlife would lose their homes," one girl near the front of the class says. "If the construction started at the end of the summer, the squirrels might not even have enough time to build a new home before winter."

Where the fuck do the squirrels in Westmount Park live, fucking condos?

"Alright," says Mrs. Enrich, "And what if they bought up an area where, after the bulldozers ploughed through, there would be less trees? Like the dog park? What type of impact could that possibly have on the environment?"

Yeah, what if they flattened the dog park? Then my dog wouldn't be able to take a proper shit where he normally does. Like near his dog swing and monkey bars. I can't wait to tell Mom that even the dogs in Westmount have a goddamn park. Or maybe the teacher is kidding?

"The point is, when the city makes a decision like this, there are lots of ripple effects that you need to consider and think about," she says.

Half the kids in the class have their hands raised. A few are even waving them. They all look eager to explain what a hardship it would be for their dogs, or sad for the squirrels to get their apartments flattened. I wonder if they get city subsidies for their housing?

"What if we think it's a good idea?" I ask. "What if we think there are reasons why the park should be flattened? Reasons maybe more important than the squirrels being able to… well, do whatever it is that squirrels do."

Everyone goes quiet. All the arms stop waving. Some of the students seem surprised that I can actually talk.

"I would be very interested in reading that essay," Mrs. Enrich says, but her voice seems to say I'm a major fuckup for thinking people matter more than squirrels. "Go ahead. Give it your best shot."

None of them seem to know that squirrels are just rats with a fluffy tail. After the bell rings I'm on my way to geography when I pass a group of girls by the bathroom. One of them snickers. At first I want to walk faster and pretend I haven't heard them. In the Point, people never look at you and snicker. If someone wants to go, they'll look right at you and say, "What the fuck are you looking at?" And then you can either walk away, or say, "I'm looking at an asshole. Why? What are you looking at?"

But in Westmount High people act like they don't want you to hear what they're saying, even though they do. They whisper something to their friends and then they all laugh.

I wait a second before turning around. The girl doesn't lose the smirk as I walk towards her. She seems to feel safe because of her four friends standing nearby. She seems to think this is going to be some kind of debate or argument between us. I'll say something, then she'll say something clever, and then her friends will all laugh. I don't say anything as I grab the front of her shirt and quickly flip her into the garbage can. She gives a little shriek as she lands upside down but doesn't even try to get out. Her friends all take a wide step back then quickly look away. A couple of hours later when I get home Mom looks angry.

"The school called. They told me you stuffed someone into a garbage can."

I don't tell Mom that the girl is actually lucky I only flipped her into the garbage can. I had considered doing more but decided not to when she acted all scared and didn't put up a fight.

"She was asking for it," I say.

"You can't shove people into fucking garbage cans! I had to fight to get you into that school. Do you want to get kicked out on your second day?"

There could be worse things.

Everybody in the Point is buzzing about the social worker that tried to steal Mrs. Cooper's husband. For months it's all anybody can talk about. A lot of people seem to think she should be chased out of the Point and never allowed to come back. Others threaten to report her. I guess Mrs. Cooper's husband is a really ugly asshole or something because everybody keeps acting so shocked that someone as smart and educated and rich and good looking as this young social worker would pick him to sleep with.

I just don't get it at all.

"Why would anybody want to steal Mrs. Cooper's husband?" I ask.

171

"An idiot social worker, that's who," says Mom. "One who's been out of McGill only two years but still should have known better."

The social worker is one of the hippies. Dad laughs when he first hears about it, saying it doesn't surprise him one bit.

"You know how big they all are on sharing everything. She probably thinks it's cool to sleep with one of her projects."

Mom doesn't seem to think it's so funny.

"Do you have any idea the kind of damage she's done? What a major set back it's created? The betrayal it represents for all of us?"

Dad snorts. "Hey, she didn't hurt me one bit. Well, except maybe my feelings a bit for picking Bob over me. Who knew the guy had it in him? She's how old? Twenty-two? Twenty-three?"

"How come everybody blames the social worker?" I finally ask Mom. "I mean, Mr. Cooper isn't a kid or anything."

Mom tries to explain how it's a violation of the people's trust and how without the people's trust that social worker won't be able to do her job.

"She took advantage," says Mom, "and she of all people should know better, should know the impact her selfish actions would have on everything we've all been working on together here for years now. She should be shot. Or at least get her stupid ass kicked back to Westmount."

Mom says this social worker knew coming into the Point that the people she'd be working with don't have any power.

"These are people without a voice, people who already lack confidence in the system."

Mrs. Cooper is really upset, especially since her husband is insisting that he and the social worker are in love. When the social worker dumps him a couple of weeks later, all the mothers are thrilled.

"I hope Anita doesn't take him back," says Mom on the phone. "She'd be a fucking idiot to let him back in the door."

But I can hear the lie in her voice. Point women always take their men back.

Chapter Nine

I QUICKLY LEARNED DURING my first few weeks at Westmount High that there's actually an art to swearing. I didn't know there was a wrong way to swear until the first time I heard a rich kid say "fuck." It's like they manage to somehow pronounce it with extra syllables, and they hesitate right before they say it. They never swear in front of teachers, either. It's usually in the hallway or cafeteria and in between classes when I hear someone swear.

"I have this stupid… fock-ing assignment in math class," I hear a girl saying to her friend as they grab their books from their lockers, lowering her voice in case any teachers are nearby, I guess. She said the 'fuck' and the 'ing' like two separate words. The girl has a bandanna wrapped around her hair, which I think is supposed to make her look tough but it looks expensive. She's wearing leather wristbands with metal studs and short leather boots with skinny heels. I'd love to punch the shit out of her. I walk by as slowly as I can, hoping she'll snicker or say something stupid to me but she must be reading the force field around my body.

Nobody in the Point tries to say fuck on purpose. It's just a word that's part of our sentences. Maybe swearing is just like learning another language—if you try to learn how to speak it past a certain age, you'll never lose your accent. My sisters and I never swear in front of our parents, of course. That would just be rude. It's sort of like smoking. Once you're old enough and your parents give you permission, like mine did when I was fifteen, you're allowed to say "fuck." Just not in front of them.

Mom's at one of her conferences again. A couple weeks ago she actually went to Vancouver for a bunch of meetings or training or something. When she got back I didn't come and see her at the door right away, waiting in my room in the upstairs landing. I wanted her to notice I wasn't there and ask, "Where's Kathy?" But after a couple minutes she still hadn't asked where I was and I was starting to feel embarrassed so I finally went down to the kitchen. When she saw me I could tell she was wondering why I hadn't run to the door to see her like everyone else. I didn't know how to explain it. Although she was in Vancouver for almost a week with some of the other people from her groups, she hasn't been doing as many of her sit-ins and protests lately. She mostly gets sent to different places now for conferences and meetings and lectures. But it was in the Point that she got to meet Senator Edward Kennedy, some important guy from the States. Mom said he came to the Point to check out our clinic and learn how we do stuff in Canada.

"If you get hit by a bus in the States," says Mom, "you better hope that you're rich. And if you get cancer you might as well jump off a bridge."

I'm not sure what this guy thinks we can teach him in the Point but when Mom came back after meeting with him at the clinic, she kept going on and on about how genuine he is.

"This guy is the real deal!" says Mom. "He genuinely cares about his country and wants to make a difference in their health care."

Then she laughs and says he isn't bad looking, either. To be honest, after watching him while he walked around the clinic, posing outside for all the news cameras and photographers, I don't see what the big deal is. Dad is way better looking.

Even though Mom isn't facing off against the riot squad or the police as much anymore, she's still been acting stressed out. I think part of it has to do with all the Peppers working at the clinic now—they're refusing to speak English in meetings. Mom speaks pretty good French, thanks to some of the courses she took at McGill, but it bugs her anyway.

"We need to work together," she says into the phone. "If we allow them to divide us then we've allowed them to make both of us weaker. They want us at each other's throats but we share a lot of common goals."

I hear Mom and Dad arguing about moving out of the Point again.

"Stop feeding me that line about it being 'hypocritical' for us to move, Eileen. You won't become part of the Establishment just because you want your kids to grow up in a better neighbourhood, for Christ's sake."

"I thought you learned from last time, Russell. You can take the kid out of the Point, but you can't take the Point out of the kid! The way to help our kids and every other kid here isn't to move. We need to fight for better schools for everyone, we need to fight for…"

"You know why I think you don't want to move, Eileen? You don't want to move because in LaSalle you wouldn't be some kind of Freedom From Poverty fighting hero. You only want to help our kids when there's a spotlight and a stage."

I hear the slap, followed by another one just a second later. Mom doesn't say anything after that. The kitchen goes real quiet and I'm afraid they're about to walk out and find me standing in the hallway, listening to them. But now it's so quiet, I can't sneak away. They'd hear the floorboards squeaking. I stand there, frozen, wishing I could levitate back up the stairs. I'm relieved when I hear my dad's voice.

"Are you crying?" He sounds worried.

It doesn't sound like Mom's voice when she says, "What the fuck am I supposed to do? Either way I lose."

"I don't know why you see it that way. Moving out of here is a win-win. I'd be back, our family would all be together, and our kids would be out of the Point."

Dad convinced Mom to move to Ville LaSalle once before but it didn't last long. It was before we went to Westmount High. The apartment we lived in was really nice, so clean and perfect, no roaches or mice or rats and there was even hot running water. Instead of an oil stove sitting in the corner, warm air rushed out of the floor from a vent. It was amazing. The Super kept asking Mom how many kids we had living there, though, while trying to sneak a peek past her in the doorway. Like maybe we'd all be lined up in the hallway for the asshole to take a head count or something. He was such a rude fucker, too.

"This isn't Point St. Charles!" he'd always say, like we didn't know we were living in LaSalle. But living in LaSalle for those few months was so weird. In the Point, everyone is the same. In LaSalle, there are all kinds of different people and the Peppers and the English don't fight with each other all the time. They just pretend not to see each other. When Dad left, Mom said he had moved back in with his mother but from the way she said it I could tell he had actually moved in with one of his girlfriends. We tried to avoid the Super as much as possible once Dad was gone but he was like the Jew from the Point. Constantly banging on our door, demanding his money.

"Your rent is late!" he'd yell at Mom as we'd walk by him in the hallway, pretending not to hear or even see him.

I bet he wouldn't have talked like that to Mom if Dad had been around.

"I know you're in there. Don't make me use my key!"

Mom finally opened the door. "I'll have the money for you tomorrow. I just spoke to my husband and he said he'd be back from his job late tonight or in the morning. So until then, fuck off!"

I'm not sure if it was the fuck off or the talk of a husband coming back from some job that made him suddenly back off and walk away, but whatever it was, it sure shut him up.

"We have to move back to the Point, anyway," Mom said that night as she stuffed our clothes and blankets and pillows into garbage bags. "I have to live in the Point if I want to keep my job with the clinic."

We went to different schools when we lived in the nice apartment in LaSalle. The kids at Cecil Newman School mostly acted like I was invisible. The teacher thought I was so dumb, I had to be faking it. Mom was interviewed by the *Gazette* after we moved back to the Point and they called her Mrs. O in the article. Ruth was all insulted because the reporter said she was a boy in the paper.

"The reporter had to pretend you were a boy so nobody would know it was us," Mom explained. "There aren't too many families with six girls."

Ruth still wasn't happy. "Why couldn't Annie or Kathy be the boy?"

Mom said the teachers at Cecil Newman were tricked because of our report cards.

"Lorne School gave you great marks," said Mom, "so of course Cecil Newman expected great things from you. But it's okay, Westmount High knows you're coming from an inner-city school."

I'm not sure what difference it makes, Westmount High knowing about us coming from an inner-city school with our fake report cards and lying Commendables. I failed every single class in grade seven but they moved me on to grade eight anyway. When I failed every class in grade eight, they just moved me on to grade nine. Mom gets a call from the school at least once a week. I'm not sure if the last one was from Mr. Henry, the math teacher, or Mr. Hilbrant, the geography teacher. When Mr. Henry asked me a question the other day I pretended to be thinking it over, touching my forehead, like if he gave me enough time to wander around in my head I'd eventually stumble across the answer. But after a couple seconds he got impatient.

Instead of asking someone else if they knew the answer, he put his hands on my desk and said, "Well?"

"Um," I tapped my forehead again, trying to pretend I was thinking.

"I don't know what you expect to find in there," Mr. Henry said, "Because it's obviously empty!"

The whole class laughed and I sat down immediately.

It was a while later, when I was staring at the clock and wishing it could go faster, when I suddenly realized the whole class was quiet. Mr. Henry had asked me another question.

"Are you even listening?"

"What?" I said.

"I said, are you even listening?"

"What?" I said again.

"I said…" Mr. Henry stopped when the class started laughing.

In geography Mr. Hilbrant handed me a pile of blank sheets of paper to pass around to the rest of the class.

"There's one for each person," he said and then turned away.

I tossed them over my shoulder and said loudly, "Hey guys, there's one for each of you."

Mr. Hilbrant opened his mouth for a second, then didn't say anything. A moment later he said, "Pay attention, people!" But the entire class was already silent, everyone just staring at him, waiting to see what he'd do.

"Come on, pick up your papers!" he finally snapped.

I left mine lying on the floor behind me. Fucker. I stared at him for the entire class but he didn't look in my direction. After that he never spoke to me again. He must have talked about me with the other teachers because now they're all ignoring me, not asking me any more questions or giving me papers to hand out. Once in a while a substitute will show up and call on me for an answer. Most of the time I just ask if I can go to the bathroom, or simply get up and leave, ignoring the substitute's insistence that I take my seat immediately. Mom says that if she gets any more phone calls, letters, or has to go to the school anymore for any reason she'll kick me out of the house. At least Dad is still on my side. Mom said she wouldn't go anymore after they kept calling and calling. The school finally said I'm not allowed to return until a parent comes with me to the office. Dad says he'll come with me, and on the drive to the school, asks me to tell him what to expect.

"I'm on your side, kiddo, no matter what. But don't let them catch me off guard in there. Tell me exactly what they're going to tell me about and I'll support you."

Dad always has my back. I don't know why he even likes Mom. All she ever does is yell and bitch at him. No wonder he doesn't want to live with us. Whenever we go into hiding now I usually find a way to call him when no one is around and let him know where we are. When we were at Nick's farm, a doctor's place in the country that one of Mom's hippie friends knows, I couldn't let Dad know how to find us because I didn't really know where we were. But Dad knows I'm on his side.

"All they're going to tell you about is the smoking," I tell Dad.

"That's it. They caught me in the bathroom with a cigarette."

I still remember the smug look on the teacher's face when she walked in and saw it in my fingers. "Come with me!" she said like she had just won the fucking lottery.

I dropped it on the floor and crushed it under my foot without even really thinking about it. The teacher made a gasping noise like she had lost her breath, staring at the crushed butt.

"Pick that up!"

"If you want it, you pick it up," I said. Was she crazy?

I tell Dad how I tried explaining to the VP that I had my parents' permission to smoke, but the VP hadn't believed me and even said I had violated a school rule.

"Yes, most schools don't want any students smoking," says Dad. "Do they have a smoking area outside?"

I hate having to admit that they do.

"So you did break a rule," says Dad. "You'll have to apologize and promise never to do that again."

When we walk into the office and I see the look on the VP's face, I instantly know the slimy fuck has something up his sleeve.

"Please sit down," he says, indicating the two armless chairs opposite his desk. I feel like we're at a job interview.

"Thank you so much for coming in Mr. Dobson. It's a pleasure to finally meet you face to face."

Dad nods. "I understand that my daughter has broken one of your rules about smoking? We've discussed it quite a bit and she completely understands why that was unacceptable."

Dad looks at me. I know it's my turn.

"Yes, I shouldn't have been smoking in the bathroom. That was wrong and stupid and I promise to never do that again."

I look at the VP but the asshole is staring at a folder on his desk in front of him. Without even looking up he says, "But we both know there's more to this than just a quick smoke in the girl's bathroom, right?"

He looks up and smiles at me. I want to smash his face.

"Right. I guess I shouldn't have put it out on the floor but to be honest, Mrs. Crooks freaked me out when she suddenly walked in and I dropped it without even thinking. Then I stepped on it so, you know, it wouldn't start a fire or anything..."

"I hadn't realized you'd done that, actually," says the VP. He looks down at the folder in front of him and taps it with his finger. "This is what we need to discuss."

Dad looks over at me. A small frown makes his forehead crease.

"You know that Kathy has been involved in numerous confrontations with the staff, other students, and almost started a race war last month when a large group of students from a different... neighbourhood showed up and practically invaded our school. I know from her file that her teachers have been as supportive as humanly possible, even allowing her to pass courses that she did practically no work in but feeling she'd..."

I tune him out. Dad knows about the gang from Little Burgundy already and he also knows it wasn't my fault. If I hadn't pushed back I would have been Wendy's bitch for the rest of my life at Westmount High.

"Who with half a brain starts a race war when they're the only one in their race standing in front of the other race?" I burst out. "That fight had nothing to do with anybody's 'race.'"

I stop talking, the angry tears fighting to get out. Wendy had also been part of the integration program. From the moment she pumped her chest out like a pigeon and told me she could kick anybody's ass from Point St. Charles or anywhere else on the planet, I knew there was going to be trouble. What else could I have done? That bitch would have been pushing me for the rest of my life. No way.

Wendy had stood looming over my desk after I sat down for science class. I had seen her a few times in the hallway and I knew she had seen me too, but we weren't in any classes together.

"Your cousin says you think you're all that but let me tell you, bitch, you get in my way anytime anywhere and we're gonna go," she said, smacking her hands down on my desk and then leaning in close. "I don't care if somebody is ten feet tall, ain't no one tells me what to do. I'll kick anybody's ass!"

"Well, asshole, I'm exactly five foot seven," I said to Wendy, her face so close to mine I could smell her shitty breath.

Her reaction surprised me. I was sure we'd go right then and there, settle it right away. Instead she took a step back and made some lame talk about what a shit school we were in and how shitty the teachers were and how stupid everything was.

"Excuse me? And who are you?" Mrs. Brenner asked when she walked into the room.

Wendy looked at her for a second before strolling out of the class, ignoring Brenner's puzzled look. The next day Wendy showed up with some kids from her neighbourhood. I could see a bunch of them standing in front of the doors of the school. I hadn't thought about Wendy since she left Mrs. Brenner's class, thinking it was over. As I walked past them and through the doors of the school they fell into step behind me. I opened my locker and pretended to be moving my books around. Wendy came walking up and slammed the locker shut. I didn't have to look to know her friends were all up close behind me now, forming a tight circle. It's what I would have done. I was dying to ask what her problem was, why she wanted to do this, but I knew the question would just make her feel stronger. More powerful.

"Like I told you bitch, I ain't afraid of anybody, anywhere!"

I couldn't help myself.

"Right. You and fifteen spares."

Wendy lunged before I could say anything else, but I'd already read that move. I had her planted up tight against the lockers when I suddenly felt the pummel of tight punches hitting my back, arms, and even the back of my head. My face hit hers, making my eyes water and then someone was pulling me back by my hair. I wished that Ruth or Annie could have been there, but Ruth had already graduated and Annie was on a work study. Annie would have had my back, and Ruth would have gone down fighting with me. Ruth might be mean and bossy sometimes, but she's the only one who can be mean and bossy with us girls. By the time the fight was over ten minutes later, I was soaked all the way through with sweat and feeling light headed, like you do after the first couple of deep ones on a fresh joint.

"Wanna let go?" It was Wendy's whispering voice in my ear. We both had a lock on each other's hair and were wedged against some desks in the back of a classroom. I don't know how we moved from the hallway into Mrs. Crooks's room, but I knew it was her classroom because I had seen a flash of her face as she ran out.

"Sure," I said. We both instantly let go.

When I stood up I saw the crowd of students, dozens of them pushing and shoving each other for a closer look. When Wendy started to walk away the crowd instantly parted. Her friends seemed to have already left. I saw Mrs. Crooks pushing her way into the room.

"Come on people, we've already lost ten minutes, I need all of you sitting down right now!" She clapped her hands. Most of the students left, some went to their desks and sat down.

"You can leave now," she said to me without even looking.

I can leave now? I looked at her. She had parked her ass at her desk and was going through a pile of papers, glaring at the late-comers who were coming through the door.

"You fucking bitch. You fucking coward." I sounded out of breath. Like I had been running for miles.

"What…?"

Mrs. Crooks looked up at me like I was on fire. Then she quickly looked away. Her metal garbage can was lying on its side next to her desk. I bent over and straightened it, then kicked it as hard as I could. It sounded like a gun going off, over and over again until it finally stopped bouncing. I left her room.

I tune back in to what the VP is saying to me and Dad in his office.

"…yes, but since you refused to discuss what exactly had happened and practically attacked a staff member, one of our most senior teachers, we could only deduce…"

"My daughter ended up with bruises all over her body and half of her hair pulled out," says Dad. "We even had to bring her to the clinic for a tetanus shot because of the bites she got, if you can believe it. I hardly…"

"Did your daughter also mention the fact that she's skipped 83 days of gym class?" says the VP. "Did you discuss that at length as well? Hmmm?"

The prick is actually smiling. I have to fight back the urge to ask the fucker if he has his dick all hard in his hand under the desk. Fucker.

"Yes, she did," says Dad.

I force myself not to look over at him. The VP frowns. Bet his dick is all limp under his desk now.

"We discussed it again on the way over here actually," says Dad. "What Kathy doesn't want you to know, but I've explained to her why it's important to share with you, is that she hates wearing gym shorts in front of the other girls. You know, she feels self-conscious."

I don't know who gave Dad the more pained look. The VP or me.

"I don't really see embarrassment as a legitimate…"

"A signed note from a parent requesting their child be excused from gym is considered a legitimate way to be excused from class though, isn't it?" Dad is smiling back at the VP.

"Do you really think that serves the best interest of your child?" asks the VP. "When a parent acts as an enabler…."

Dad stands up. "I can put it in writing now or I can send in a note with Kathy later but as far as I'm concerned, she's no longer required to attend any gym classes. Let her know if she needs to attend the library or sit in the office and read a book or something during the period but she won't be going to gym anymore. Now if you'll excuse me, I have to get to work. I've taken up enough of your valuable time. Thank you for meeting with us."

As we walked out of the office, I knew not to give the VP a triumphant finger behind Dad's back.

"I thought I asked you to come clean with me and tell me everything," Dad says as he backs his car out of the school's parking lot.

I had actually completely forgotten about gym since I haven't been to class in months.

"I'm sorry, Dad, I didn't know he was going to say anything about gym. I'd forgotten all about it until he…"

"Yeah, that's what bothered me," says Dad. "That look of 'got you!' on his face just bugged me."

"Thanks, Dad. I didn't mean to lie."

Dad looks over at me and smiles. "Some things are more important than the truth."

When we get home I know not to say anything to Mom. She'd probably take a fit about me cutting so many classes. She doesn't understand stuff like Dad does. Mom probably isn't even lying when she says she used to love school.

"I loved going to class and learning. I was a good student. School was my favourite place when I was a kid. I was never more sad than when I was forced to quit. I wish I could have finished my education."

Maybe I wouldn't hate school if I was a good student. Mom used to get straight A's in everything except for 'Personal Hygiene.'

Mom says I have to start seeing a doctor at the clinic for an hour each week.

"It's just so you can talk about whatever's bugging you with someone who is a really good listener," says Mom. "Someone neutral."

"But what would I tell him?" I can't believe she's going to make me talk to some fucking stranger. A man stranger.

"You can talk about whatever you want," says Mom. "How it's going at school, how you feel about school…"

I know it's complete bullshit. What about Uncle Luther? Or maybe Uncle Eddy? Or Grandpa? Or the pervert at the end of Liverpool Street? Can I talk about what a fucking hypocrite my mother is? Making me talk to some complete stranger about anything and everything except for any of our family secrets, of course. Only talk about the shit that makes Mom look like a hero. She wants to drag me into the clinic to be a guinea pig again. So I get to be the first headcase and official psycho in the Point? Fucking great.

"Can I talk about…anything?"

Mom gives me a strange look.

"Of course," she says with a small smile.

Oh really?

"Can I can tell him about… you-know-what?"

Mom whirls on me. "You little troublemaker, what the hell is wrong with you? Why are you so goddamn confrontational all the time?"

Yeah. Just what I thought.

"Confrontational? Coming from you? You're just a big fake, a fucking hypocrite!"

Mom and I have a lot of screaming matches but somehow this one seems worse than usual.

"You're going to push your luck too far one of these days, you know that?" she says. "And then what are you going to do, eh? Don't push me, Kathy. Just don't push me."

I know to shut up.

When I meet the doctor for the first time he tells me to call him Elliot. I'm not even sure he's a real doctor. I sit across his huge brown desk in a black leather chair and try to hate him on the spot. It's hard.

"Anything said in this room stays in this room," he says.

For the first month or so I tell him as much bullshit and lies as I can come up with. My grandmother is torturing my Aunt Mary, slowly poisoning her and stealing her government cheque each month. My dad is a hitman with the Irish gang. My Uncle Patrick killed his first wife and my Aunt Olive is his only mistake and he doesn't undo it as he likes the constant reminder of how booze can ruin your life. I was adopted at birth and my parents broke up because my mom wanted to give me back to my birth parents but my dad disagreed. Oh, and my sister Ruth is a vampire who was fucked by the Devil one night. Okay, so maybe some of it was true. But Elliot seems to believe every single thing I tell him. I can't help but love him a little.

"Why don't we focus on school during tonight's session," he says. "What if you were to tell me how it's going at Westmount

High School?"

Fuck.

"It's okay," I say.

"I have one rule here," says Elliot, "and that's we always tell the truth, okay? If you don't want to talk about something and you say so, that's fair. But don't tell me everything at school is 'fine' when we both know that's not true."

I decide against telling Elliot that sometimes you have to lie to tell the truth.

"I hate school," I finally say. "But everybody hates school."

"Why do you hate it?" asks Elliot. "I didn't hate school. I actually enjoyed school."

What in the hell do you say to that?

"Well I'm glad you liked school, Elliot. That's nice. Very nice. Bet you had lots of friends and got great marks and the teachers all loved you and everything."

I'm surprised when I realize during a session that I like having someone to tell some of my secrets to.

"You have so many secrets," says Elliot.

"But even more lies," I say with a smile.

I debate whether to tell him how in my family, with five sisters, each of us has a specific role. Ruth is bossy, still kind of Nanny's girl. Annie IS the boss, Julia is Mom's favourite, Beth is funny, and Hannah is the baby. Me? I'm the liar and the troublemaker. Before I can tell him, Elliot asks me a question.

"When do you think you'll feel ready to talk about it?"

For a second I wonder if I missed something. When I realize what he's up to, before he can say another word, I'm shaking my head.

"No," I say. "Don't."

Elliot smiles at me but his eyes look sad. I want to run out of his office but I hope if I don't move he'll understand and not say another word.

"If you want to utterly destroy a child," he says, "rob them of their soul in one single act, first sexually abuse them. Then call them a liar."

I miss our next session. And the next. Elliot finally calls me.

"I'd like you to come to our next session, Kathy," says Elliot. "I'd like to talk to you."

When I say sure, no problem, he laughs.

"Don't say you'll come when you know you won't. I can't have you not showing up week after week, letting me save that time for you and then have you not using it. I'm going to save our time for next week. I have you on my schedule. Please come."

He's smart. At our next meeting he doesn't say anything about school. Or lies. Or children missing their souls. He doesn't ask me any questions. He just lets me talk about anything I want to. I tell him how unfair my mom is to my dad. How she never has anything happy or nice to say and how all she does is complain and tell him what a terrible provider and father and husband he is and then wonders why he doesn't want to live with us.

"I know you all think she's some kind of a hero around here," I say, "but she's not. She's a total fake."

"You sound angry with your mother," says Elliot.

"What else is new?" I say. "We're always mad at each other."

Elliot picks up his pen. Then sets it back down. "Are you angry about anything else?"

I guess this is when I'm supposed to fall apart and start sobbing about school and say I'm a complete fuck up and have no friends and I'm failing every course. Which is pretty much the truth but what would be the point of saying any of that shit?

"My mom said you're going to test my sister, Annie," I say.

It's because of Annie's English teacher that she has to get tested. Mrs. Crooks is a bully. I hate the bitch.

Elliot looks away for a minute.

"Yes, I'm meeting with her tomorrow afternoon."

"She wants me to come with her," I say. It's the only reason why I showed up for our session. "Annie gets real nervous before tests and she thinks she'll do better if I was with her."

"There's no way that can happen," says Elliot. "These tests have to be administered with no distractions and in complete privacy. You being there is simply out of the question."

I know better than to beg. Instead, I play my trump card.

"She won't show up if you don't let me come with her," I say calmly. "Point girls don't like being alone with men they don't know. Strange men."

Elliot grins. "Am I that strange?"

I can hardly wait for Annie to meet him. She knows I love him. Trust him. She doesn't know what secrets I've told him but she knows I don't think he's a pig.

"He talked about his wife one time," I tell Annie. "I think he thought it would make me feel safer."

We both laugh at that. Only a man would think that would make a girl feel safe. Yet somehow it did.

The next day, after Elliot smiles at Annie and shakes her hand, I try not to feel jealous. I don't want him to like her more than me. After she sits down, he looks over at me.

"It's crucial that you not say a word," he says. "You can sit over there."

My chair is at the back of the room, to the side. I open my book right away and pretend to read. Elliot spends the next half hour asking her all kinds of stupid questions and showing her pictures and having her pick A or B. Rich people must know a lot of shit about nothing, crap that no one really cares about anyway. Maybe if we had a TV that worked and had more than just channel six we'd all know a bunch of useless stuff, too. I'm pretty good through most of the test and lame questions, sitting quietly, not making a sound. I know Annie feels better and worse for having me there. A part of her likes knowing I'm just across the room, close enough to help her if things go wrong. But also close enough to witness her bomb, something she always worries about when it comes to taking a test. I feel a little bad for not having told her the truth, that within minutes of meeting Elliot she'd feel okay about being alone with him. But I had wanted to be there and watch him with another person. I wanted to see how much of what he does with me is fake.

"Where is Chile found?" asks Elliot.

What a fucked up question. I mean really, unless you're a geography teacher or some fucking genius or a kid from Westmount, how would you know where the fuck Chile is found?

"On a hotdog," says Annie.

For a second, it doesn't register. Then my brain catches up and before I can stop myself I'm laughing so hard I think I'm going to pee my pants.

"That's enough, Kathy," says Elliot. "Settle down."

"On a hotdog? Chile is found on a hotdog? Oh fuck me, Annie! A HOTDOG?" Then I start laughing again.

"Where else would it be?" says an indignant Annie.

"He means where in the world is Chile—the country!" I manage to choke out.

Annie looks stricken. "You don't know where it is either," she says.

"I know it's not on a fucking hotdog!"

The funny thing is, I'm pretty sure we've never even had chili before anyway. My sisters and me agree that it looks like sick dog shit. Like some alley hound had been rummaging around in somebody's garbage and then shit it all back out in a bowl.

Elliot stands in front of me. "I need you to leave. I need you to leave right now. I knew this was a bad idea from the beginning. I can't believe I allowed myself to be talked into this. Seriously, you need to go. Right now."

I've never seen Elliot so upset. I think he's really starting to hate me. Annie refuses to speak to me for the rest of the day. For days I can't help myself. Every once in a while I look at her and grin and she instantly says, "Shut up. Okay? Just shut up."

Even after Mom triumphantly calls the school, demanding an appointment so she can share Annie's test results, Annie seems to think the tests prove she's dumb or something. I'm dying to ask her what she thinks of Elliot. Does she think he's cute?

"Mrs. Crooks really hates me," says Annie. "She's always asking me in front of the whole class if I'm stupid or something."

"Did she actually use the word stupid?" I ask.

"No, says Annie. "She asked me if I'm retarded."

When Mrs. Crooks sees me smoking near the lockers in the basement a few days later, at first I almost drop my butt to the floor. Then I force myself to lock eyes with her and take a deep haul. Let the bitch report me again. She looks away and then disappears around a corner. For the first time in my life there's a teacher I actually want to have.

At school this morning a teacher I don't even have stops me in the hallway.

"Hey, you're from Point St. Charles, right?"

How can they always tell?

"Yeah."

"Do you know anything about Sharron Prior?"

Sharron Prior? She hadn't even been a student at Westmount High. She was a year older than me and they just found her body in a field in Longueil. She'd been raped and beaten, her face covered with bruises, a tooth knocked out where the bastard had punched her, and her chest caved in where he had kneeled until she choked on her own blood. Her jeans and underwear were found about six feet from her body. The article in the *Gazette* said she might have been alive after the killer or killers left her there to die. There was speculation she had been held captive for a day or two before they dumped her body in the field. I remember all of us looking for her, searching the parks and near the train tracks, hoping she was just another runaway. Mom was pretty sure something bad had happened to her though, saying everyone who knew the family said she was a great kid, very close to her mother and her brother and sisters.

"She never would have run away," said Mom.

I look at the teacher. "Nope, never heard of her."

The teacher walks away without saying another word. Later that day in home economics Mrs. Maguire tells us we're making cookies for our favourite teacher.

"Pick a partner and then both of you need to agree which teacher to make the cookies for. Then we'll hunt them down, wherever they are, and present them!"

She says that like we'll be handing over bars of fucking gold to the lucky winners instead of homemade shit by kids with dirty hands and at least one of them without a fucking clue about how to make anything worth eating.

I lean over to the kid sitting next to me and say softly, "Fucking teachers will eat anything if it's free, eh?"

The kid looks startled. "Uh, I already have a partner," she says.

When Mrs. Maguire sees me working alone, pouring half a bag of chocolate chips into a huge bowl with flour and other shit I'd read on the handout that needs to be added, she asks me what I'm doing.

"I'm doing what you think I'm doing," I say.

The class goes silent.

"I see a student working on their own, using double the amount of one ingredient, and obviously not paying attention to any of the directions which were explicitly…"

She stops talking as I walk away. "And where do you think you're going?" she demands.

"To find my favourite teacher!" I say.

It's weird to be on the bus going home so early. There's hardly anyone else on.

"I'm so sick and tired of the goddamn school calling me every single fucking day," says Mom that night.

"Then let me quit, " I say for the millionth time. "I could get a job and pay you room and board and then you wouldn't have to listen to the school anymore!"

When Mom doesn't say anything I look over at her. She looks like she's actually considering it.

"Maybe that isn't such a bad idea," she says. "If I sign the papers you could leave even before your sixteenth birthday. What's the point of having you registered as a student when you never go to class, never do any homework, and scare half the teachers to death. Even Elliot says you're just wasting his time. You aren't even on his schedule anymore."

Scare half the teachers to death? Elliot doesn't want to see me anymore?

"Which teachers are afraid of me?" I demand. I didn't know half the teachers had even noticed me. Afraid of me? Why?

"If you want to quit, I won't stand in your way," says Mom. "I'm sick of fighting about it. I'm done."

"No, seriously, which teachers?" I ask. Did this mean I wouldn't see Elliot anymore? Ever? Didn't I have to be a student to keep going for the sessions each week?

But Mom isn't listening anymore. Ever since the clinic started paying her it's like instead of being mad at the city or school board or welfare office, now she's always mad at us. At me.

The next morning I wake up with a start. It's almost nine o'clock and no one woke me up. I rush to the kitchen and find Mom sitting at the table, smoking a Player's and drinking a cup of coffee. All my sisters have already left for school. It's just Mom and I.

"I called the school," she says. "You win, you don't have to go back. They agreed I could sign you out even though you won't be sixteen yet for a while. I think they even agree it's a good idea, to be honest. They're as fed up with you and your bullshit as I am."

I don't have to go to school anymore? I won? What did I win?

"You serious?" I ask.

"Yes, Vivian is being switched to the night shift this week and needs a babysitter for the kids to sleep over. I told her you could start tomorrow. Just get to her place by six."

Mom finally looks up at me.

"What? Oh for Christ sake, don't you start!" she says. "This is exactly what you've been wanting only now you're actually going to be paid to skip school and do nothing all fucking day. It's not like you're going to get your hand stuck in some meat grinder working at the corner store like that kid in Verdun who just had four of his fucking fingers ripped off last week. You'll even get to sleep on the job. Once her kids go to bed at nine or so you can sleep. She'll wake you up in the morning when she gets home. You'll make enough to buy your own smokes now and have enough left over to save up for some real jeans in just a month or so. The rest you can give to me for your room and board."

I'm not a student anymore. I have a job. I'm going to make money. I'm finally going to have a pair of jeans. Real jeans. Brand new even. So why do I feel so sick?

"But… Mom…" She won't look at me. "Do you really think that's such a good idea?" I ask.

I don't know what else to say, but I know once I leave that room, once I let Mom leave the kitchen, there will be no turning back. I don't want to go to school. But I don't not want to, either.

"What do you mean, do I think it's a good idea?" asks Mom. "Since when do you give a flying fuck what I think?"

Mom and I have been banging heads for a long time now. I'm always telling her that she's a fake and a hypocrite. She's always telling me that I'm way too confrontational and just a lying troublemaker. I can't wrap my brain around the idea that I'm not a student anymore. Can a person still become a writer if they drop out of high school?

"But I thought you said that without an education, a person's life is just shit," I say.

Mom gives a short mean sounding laugh.

"I think your life is officially shitty anyway, right? So what's one more piece of shit?"

Well fuck me. I leave the kitchen and go upstairs. I sit on my bed on the landing and stare out the window at the Redpath Sugar sign for a while. Then I look away. The tears want to fall but something's wrong, like my eyes are too small or something. I can't even cry right.

Fuck that.

I'll find a way. Somehow I'll find a way. The fuckers. I look back at the Redpath Sugar sign. I wonder if there's a kid somewhere in Westmount who can see it outside their bedroom window, too. I wonder if it looks different to them, since I'm looking up and they're looking down.

Chapter Ten

I'VE NEVER UNDERSTOOD the point of cleaning a toilet. The first time someone takes a shit it's dirty again, so why bother unless you're going to clean it after every shit? Besides, isn't that what flushing is for? I don't know anyone in the Point who does anything more than that. But my summer job at Camp Amy Molson includes bathroom duty every four days like the rest of the staff. When Brynn Cameron asked me to clean the toilets, she handed me a pair of yellow gloves, a huge container of Ajax, and a big brush on a long skinny pole. She was obviously expecting more than just a couple of flushes.

"You need to really get in there," says Brynn.

Really get in there? Why not just hand me a biohazard suit and a pair of fucking goggles, then I could just step right in and give it a really good going over. If Brynn wasn't the assistant director of the camp, I might have told her to go fuck herself, thinking she must be messing with me. But after spending more than two years babysitting, working in nursing homes, and a short stint at McDonald's since dropping out of grade nine, I know I'm lucky to be working at Camp Amy Molson for the entire summer.

"And don't forget under the rim," says Brynn.

I look down at the giant toothbrush in my hand and suddenly the rubber gloves make sense. Brynn is still standing next to me, waiting for me to start. After pulling on the gloves, the toothbrush handle feels like a skinny penis shoved into a loose condom. It's hard to get a good grip and it doesn't help having Brynn standing so close, watching my every move.

"Uh, I think I got it now," I say.

Brynn looks at me for a second, seems to change her mind about something, and then finally leaves. After I sprinkle some of the Ajax shit on the inside of the toilet bowl, I feel like an idiot scrubbing it with the toilet brush. I hope no one shows up to take a dump while I'm still in there. During staff orientation the camp director warned us that we'd all be taking turns cleaning both the staff and camper bathrooms. With 150 campers and 85 staff shitting and pissing in the bathrooms every single day, we have to stay on top of stuff.

"You almost done?" Brynn has come back to check my work.

"Yup," I say, moving back for her to have a look.

"Great! I'll take those," she says, reaching for the Ajax and disgusting brush now leaning against the wall. I watch as she places it all into a shelving unit along the wall and then locks it up.

"You can never be too careful," she says with a smile.

I realize she means with the campers, not me stealing the stuff.

"Uh, right. Of course."

I hate how stupid I always sound around Brynn but she makes me a nervous wreck. I'm always worried she can tell I have a major crush on her. I don't mean I want to lick her muff or anything, just maybe sit at her feet and listen while she talks. I'd guess her to be in her mid-twenties. She wears the same kind of T-shirt every single day. Dark navy with yellow stripes one day, deep burgundy with green stripes the next. Then black with red stripes just to shake things up, I guess. I've tried to find out as much about her as possible and I'm not surprised when I learn she's a psychology major. She's smart like that. When she asked me during my first interview with her what I was planning on taking in university eventually, I liked that she assumed I'd be going to university one day, too. Just like her.

"Oh, probably psychology," I said all casual.

Fuck. I'm so lame. Like she's going to instantly sit up and notice me and want to hang out with me because, hey, I want to do the same courses that she did. I might have to kill myself.

To be honest, I don't mind cleaning the camp's toilets. Not only do I get to see Brynn, who seems to be in charge of making sure the toilets are done perfectly, but anything is better than the shit jobs I've been doing since leaving school. I always hate it when camp is finished for another summer.

When I get back home, babysitting Vivian's six-year-old twins five nights a week is fun at first. Until her younger brother Fred starts sniffing around, trying to talk me up and asking me personal questions all the time.

"You got a boyfriend? You must, right? A pretty girl like you."

Within weeks the asshole is asking me what size bra I wear, if I'm a natural blonde, and bumping into me all the time, "accidentally" pressing up against me if I happen to reach for something and he's nearby.

"Here you go," he says, handing me the coffee mug or kettle.

I keep Vivian's kids up as late as possible, trying to avoid being alone with him. Sometimes they fall asleep on the floor in front of the TV.

"Come here," says Fred one night, patting the spot on the couch next to him.

I had smelt the beer on his breath when he first arrived.

"Come on," he says with a smile. "I've got some weed."

I look at the sleeping bodies on the floor.

"I gotta get the kids into bed," I say, then start pushing their bodies with my foot. I know not to bend over with Fred behind me.

"Come on guys," I say, gently pushing on their small arms until one of them finally stirs.

"Fred says you have a crush on him," Vivian says with a sly grin after she pays me that week.

"Did my mother tell you yet?" I say. "I can't work for you anymore. Ruth got me a job at her nursing home and I need to start really soon."

I've never seen Vivian look so angry.

"And that's it? How do you expect me to find someone on such short notice?"

I can't look her in the face. "Why don't you ask Fred to watch them? He's here almost every night, anyway. You know, just until you find someone else."

I'm surprised when Mom doesn't ask me about it. Ruth doesn't ask me any questions either, and even promises to talk to somebody about maybe getting me in at her place. Within a few days, I'm scraping shit off the floor and rinsing oatmeal out of plastic bowls. I'm thrilled.

"I'm making almost double what I did with Vivian!" I say to Mom as I pass over my cheque.

She nods but doesn't say anything. I know she's distracted. She's thinking of leaving the clinic. She says the tensions between the English and French are getting worse every day.

"Today they announced, in French, that they'd be speaking only in French at all staff meetings from now on. They're trying to push us out Russ, I know it! After all we did together, they want us out! I swear to god, I'm having a nervous breakdown. I can't take much more of this."

But I know she's even more worried about how we'll handle having no money again.

"Your mental health is worth more than dollars and cents," says Dad.

He's moved back in and this time it looks like he'll be staying. His suggestion about Mom's mental health must have stuck because soon she's on a long-term disability leave from the clinic. It includes full pay.

"Now we can afford to leave the Point," argues Dad, "and they can't fire you for not living down here if you're on disability!"

Dad is such a genius. Mom tries fighting it a bit, saying she'd miss her friends and without her work in the Point, what in hell will she do in Ville LaSalle?

"I think I should go back and try again," says Mom. "How can I give that up? They need me, and my French is getting better every day…"

"You just like being a big fish in a small pond," says Dad.

After six months of working at the nursing home, I start having fantasies about going back to high school. Anything has to be better than cleaning shit off the floor where the zombies sometimes drop their load on their way back to bed, after moving the over-sized spoons around in their bowls for half an hour, sipping cold tea and gumming their dry toast. Sometimes one of the old ladies will forget and come to the table almost naked, her long tits tucked into her underwear.

"Hey you," says Ruth, "come with me sweetheart," and she'll gently guide them back to their room and help them get dressed.

If it was up to me, they could sit around naked all day, like the scary ghosts they are. Ruth is even kind when one of the old guys fondles her passing ass.

"Excuse me, Mister?" Ruth says, stopping dead in her tracks, hands on her hips. "Is that any way to treat a lady?"

Then she adds, "Oh wait, I forgot, I'm no lady!"

It always draws a huge laugh. The old people's eyes all light up as soon as Ruth enters the room.

"Mrs. Henderson, your feet are getting too cold!" says Ruth as she massages the pale blue wooden blocks with thick talons on each wrinkled toe. "You have to keep these socks on, okay?"

I knew I wouldn't last. For a long time I'm invisible, just quietly moving from room to room, picking up the pissy sheets and nightgowns, stuffing them into the large washing machine in the basement. No one but Ruth ever speaks to me and even then, Ruth will almost whisper.

"You can take your break, Kathy," she'll breathe into my ear.

I find a spot just outside the building to huddle with my smokes. I can usually inhale three within my break time unless some chirpy asshole tries to join me.

"Hey, it's a cold one today, isn't it?"

I've learned that if I stare at them for just a second longer than I should, then look away, they'll leave me alone from then on.

"Why does everyone keep saying your sister is so unfriendly?" Ruth finally asks me.

"Which sister?" I say, then smile.

Next I try getting a job at Bell Telephone.

"Just remember not to say that you don't know any French," warns my cousin Meghan.

She's been working there for four years already and says they don't hire anybody unless you know somebody already on the inside, so I'm grateful she's letting me put her name on my application.

"And they won't care that I didn't finish high school?" I ask.

"Likes I already told ya," says Meghan, "nobody on my floor finished high school. It's just bullshit work, anyways, winding wire and making sure the coils don't get all mixed up."

I know Meghan thinks it's easy work but I'm not so sure. Winding wire? Keeping coils all organized?

"Just remember to say you can speak a bit of French. They get you to pick a number between 1 and 10. Picking a one means fuck off and go away, picking a ten means you get to run the goddamn place. So pick a four or a five. And practice saying a few things before you get there."

When I get a call a few days later for an interview I'm shocked. An interview seems so serious. So grownup.

"*Bonjour*," says the woman in a dark jacket and shocking white hair. She's too young to have hair that white. I wonder if she dyes it like that on purpose. Why would anyone want to look old on purpose?

"Uh, *oui*," I say. "*Bon-jour*."

"*Parlez-vous français?*" she asks.

"*Un peu*," I say with what I hope is a winning smile. Or at least a please-fucking-hire-me smile.

"I see here you checked a level four for your French?" she says.

I'm startled to realize she's speaking in English. She doesn't even have an accent.

"Well, I'm not a big believer in exaggerating myself," I say.

Annie had warned me to act humble.

"Don't put on any airs," she said. "Don't pretend to be more than you are. That'll just make you look silly and you won't get any job doing anything, anywhere."

I know Annie is right but if Meghan is more right, admitting my French level is closer to a zero than a four would have meant not even making it to an interview.

"*Pouvez-vous me parler un peu de vous-même?*" the white haired woman asks with a smile that doesn't reach her eyes. "*Quelle expérience avez-vous dans ce domaine, pourquoi voulez-vous travailler pour cette organisation?*"

Then she leans back from her desk like she knows she's going to enjoy this. Messing with me. But of course I have to try. Even if I have no clue what the hell she just asked me.

"Uh, *oui?*" I say, figuring I have a fifty-fifty chance of being right.

She actually laughs. Then sits back up close to the desk.

"Well, you must understand that this isn't going to work," she says. "You absolutely need a minimum level of at least conversational French."

I wish I could have bragged to Annie later that I immediately stood up and after yanking my lying application out of the bitch's hands, told her in perfect French what she could do with her fake old lady hair. Instead, I look at her beautiful hands, both resting on the edge of the desk. Her long nails are painted a soft pink. I can smell her perfume from my perch opposite her wide desk. I hate having to look up. I know my face is burning. In the end I don't have to say anything.

"*Merci et au revoir,*" she says. "Have a good day."

Then she looks down at the next file folder. I know I'm finished and allowed to leave now.

"Why don't we join the fucking army?" I say to Annie that night in bed.

We're sharing the bottom bunk and eating cherry Freezies, shivering under the blankets.

"They feed you, give you a trade, and even pay you while you learn. You get all your clothing for free, even your underwear and socks, and you don't have to figure out where to live because everyone lives together in a huge barracks, like fucking family, while learning it all together!"

Annie isn't convinced.

"But what if we have to shoot somebody?" she says.

Leave it to Annie to find the fatal flaw.

"Well fuck that," I say. "You just shoot at the air above their head or you shoot them in a non-vital part. You wouldn't really kill anybody of course."

"What's a non-vital part?" asks Annie.

"You know, like a leg or an arm or a fucking eyebrow or something. Hell, I don't know!"

"An eyebrow?" says Annie with a grin.

We laugh for the next half hour, speculating about non-vital body parts, debating which parts of our own body, if we had to choose, we'd let someone shoot.

"Look, you probably wouldn't even have to ever touch a gun," I say. "With your nursing program from Westmount High they'll have you working with sick people."

"So instead of me having to shoot anyone, I'll be helping other people who have been shot? Like a soldier-nurse?" says Annie. And that's when I know I almost have her.

Since graduating from Westmount High Annie has been having a problem getting a job in nursing. Before she can get work she has to have her nursing license, but before she can get her license she has to write some huge test, all in French. Annie's French is about as good as mine. Meaning she doesn't have a hope in hell of passing some test, especially a really hard test like the nursing one is supposed to be, all in French. I guess they don't want any English nurses in Quebec. Or Bell workers.

The next day we're down at the recruiting office, sitting on a hard bench in a wide hallway, watching dozens of real soldiers walk by. I can't get over how cute some of them are, even with the goofy short haircuts. When one of them smiles at me, I can't help but grin back. Holy shit. There are a lot of hot guys in the army. I hadn't considered that angle yet. Get paid to learn a trade while meeting tons of cute guys? Guys who have real jobs and goals? With huge arms? And tight asses?

"Maybe they keep all the fat, old ugly ones in back," whispers Annie, but I can tell she's impressed too.

Neither of us have a real boyfriend yet and I'm secretly convinced

I'll be dying a virgin. All of my friends already have boyfriends but their rules are different from mine. I mean, the way I figure it is, why should I have to give a blow job to some guy on a regular basis just because I'm officially his girlfriend, just so no one else is allowed to hit on me or try and cop a feelie if they manage to corner me alone? Fuck that. I'll take care of myself, thank-you-very-much. My friend Helen has decided she'll suck off the first guy who asks her out, just so long as he has a car. Or at least one he can borrow sometimes. But my rules are a bit more strict. Number one, the guy has to be unrelated. He also has to be no more than five years older than me, know to brush his fucking teeth every day, have a job—a real job—and not believe in hitting girls. Which means I won't be dating anybody from the Point any time soon. Which means I'll be dying a virgin.

"You're just being picky," says Helen.

I know she thinks I'm just putting on airs, like I think I'm too good for normal guys. But I just know there isn't anything in it for me to pair up with anybody I've met so far. I don't need to be somebody's bitch and end up pregnant within six months, then popping out another one every year like Mom did. Nope. I'm going to die an old maid like Aunt Mary. Hopefully not insane like her, but then again, maybe that's what made her nuts? Nanny always said Aunt Mary never constituted her marriage on her wedding night, which Annie explained to me later means Aunt Mary never fucked her own husband even once before leaving him.

"Her vagina is probably all collapsed into itself by now. Dry as dust."

Maybe one of these cute soldiers walking by can help me avoid having a dried up old bird all my life. One of them suddenly stops in front of us, a clipboard in his hand.

"You can come in now," he says, pointing towards an opened doorway a few feet from our bench in the hallway.

I can't believe our luck. It looks like he's going to interview us at the same time.

"Grab a seat girls," he says with a friendly smile, pointing to the two chairs opposite his small desk.

After we settle ourselves, he taps the papers in front of him.
"So you two are sisters, right?"

We nod together.

"Which one is the nurse?"

Annie clears her throat. "Well, I guess you mean me but I'm not licensed yet so…"

Shit. I want to smack her.

"I know, I know," Mr. Friendly says while nodding at her approvingly. "Don't worry about that. We'd offer you additional training, anyway."

I've never seen Annie look so happy. Her face is a bright pink. Then he looks at me and frowns.

"Why didn't you finish high school? You've really tied my hands here. Your options are very limited."

No friendly smile or approving nod for me. I'm someone who has run out of options. He looks back down at his folder.

"Hmmm, let's see. You might get in as a weapons tech…"

What? A weapons what?

"What's that?" I ask, leaning forward. Please, don't let Annie get in and leave me behind.

Mr. Friendly spends quite a bit of time explaining what exactly a weapons tech person is and although I'm smiling and nodding, I already know I won't be dating any of those cute guys with their short haircuts and tight butts any time soon. All the good parts about being in the army are apparently crammed into that 30- second commercial, the one where a gorgeous looking navy officer is standing at the front of a huge ship in a crisp white uniform. I've already imagined signing myself up and standing at the front of that ship. Next to that seriously gorgeous navy guy, wearing a matching hat. All that's left to do is share a tent with a dozen people who aren't my sisters and get shrieked at by someone that isn't my mom. Right.

"Have either of you ever done any illicit drugs?" asks Mr. Friendly, suddenly all official.

"Of course not!" says Annie at the exact same time that I ask, "Does grass count?"

"Uh, yes, marijuana is an illegal substance and therefore 'counts.'"

Mr. Friendly has suddenly become Mr. Lieutenant Asshole. I decide it would be unfair to Annie to pretend to check my side pocket to see if my baggie is sticking out. Do they really never smoke up in the army? Don't they all get drunk every weekend? Mr. Lieutenant Asshole suddenly becomes Mr. Friendly again.

"So you girls need to think it over, very carefully, and if you're sure, just drop by again."

I think he's done when he suddenly looks at me and winks.

"Just remember, you have never, ever, engaged in any illicit activities. Which includes ALL drugs, of course. Got it?"

I resist the urge to turn my hand into a fake pistol and say, "Got it!" then blow away the imaginary smoke. Instead I keep my big mouth shut while Annie gives her excited thank you's and good-byes and see-you-soon shit. As we leave the building, I can't help sneaking one last look at all the hunks walking around, looking busy and important. Maybe all the ugly ones really are stuck back at the training base in Halifax.

A few nights before she leaves, Annie admits she's scared to death. Like I didn't already know that.

"What if no one likes me?" she cries. "What if people are mean? Or think I'm stupid?"

I know there's no way everyone isn't going to love her. But she won't believe me.

"Hey, just think of all those guys you're going to meet," I say. "Shit, you'll probably fall in love the first week and end up married to some army guy!"

She just shakes her head. "At least I'll get to help Mom and Dad."

The day Annie leaves is the worst in my entire life. I won't go to the train station with her. Dad has never been more proud of any of us.

"When you get back," he says to her, "you'll get to go to the Legion with me as a full-fledged member instead of just an auxiliary member!"

Oh joy.

As the car pulls away, I force myself to watch her face through the window. It's my punishment for having ever put the idea of the fucking army in her head in the first place.

A few weeks later I have my first official boyfriend.

"Want to dance?"

I look up. At least he's the right age. I'm tired of all the old guys at the Legion trying to make me dance with them just so they can press their hard dicks up against me. The last time Mr. Anderson did it, with all the other bodies crowded around us on the dance floor, I decided to push back. I was surprised when he pulled away and brought me back to my seat. From then on I knew what to do. For a while it was fun knowing they were all afraid of me. Mr. Anderson must have made me sound like quite the horny bitch.

"Well, do you? Wanna dance?"

I smile and stand up. I quickly learn all about Zack. He's just a year older than me and in his first year at college. His father is some big shot in the Legion and they're visiting for some meeting being held after the dance. I just smile and do a lot of nodding. I like the sound of his voice. It's soft, even hesitant. We're the exact same height. We could do it standing up. We dance every single dance until they yell for Last Call at the bar.

"Can I call you later?" he asks. I want to smile at the anxiousness in his voice.

"Sure," I say.

As he writes down my number I can see his hand shaking a bit. It makes me like him more. He's nervous.

"So I can call you, right?" he asks again.

When I smile and say "Yes," he shoves my number into his pocket and then hesitates. I know what he's thinking. After I kiss him, I turn and walk away. I know we'll be a couple real soon.

"What in the hell do you see in that guy?" demands Helen after she meets him briefly at the bus stop. "You know he's a fag, right?"

Of course I know he's gay. Or at least very confused.

"You don't know that!" I say to Helen, pretending to be offended on my new boyfriend's behalf.

But that's what makes him the perfect boyfriend. He doesn't want to fuck me. That, and he's smart. Hell, he's going to college. For the next six months we see each other every single weekend. I know not to go near the Point with him because he'd get his head kicked in within seconds of anyone spotting him. Sometimes we just sit in Pigeon Park near the metro, holding hands, and me listening to him talk.

"I have to get some gloves for winter," says Zack in his soft and hesitant voice. "I need a new pair so badly it's not even funny!"

Sometimes we'll lean our faces against each other and pretend to kiss, our lips gently touching. One time I slipped him the tongue and he pulled away in shock. Or horror. Or maybe both. When we go to St. Joseph's Oratory on the mountain he's amazed I've never been there before. It's so beautiful. Zack must have already been there a million times because he tells me all kinds of facts about the place as we walk around.

"It's the largest church in Canada," brags Zack like he owns the place.

One room is filled with thousands of old crutches, all stockpiled from when some old priest performed miracles on the cripples who used to hobble around on them. When he brings me to the museum inside, there's a shrine holding some dead guy's heart in it. I'm ready to go.

"It's Brother André's heart," says Zack. "He asked that they store it here as a form of protection for the basilica." I don't even want to ask what the "basilica" is. Sounds like some dead Italian guy's balls or something.

"You want to go now?" I ask, hoping he'll get the hint.

On our way into the church there had been a bunch of people crawling up the steps outside on their hands and knees. Zack had claimed they were hoping for a miracle.

"It's a sign of their respect. Their devotion. Some of the older ones take all day before they finally make it to the top."

I think that's totally fucked up but don't want to sound rude. When I ask Nanny about it later she says St. Joseph's is a Catholic church. Like that explains everything. I figure we should get going soon before any of them finally reach the top. But Zack has one more stop he wants us to make. In the gift shop, Zack buys me a charm bracelet. Ten tiny golden pages, each engraved with one of the Ten Commandments.

"My dad keeps saying he wants to meet you," says Zack as he attaches the bracelet to my wrist, my first gift from any boy, ever. "He's dying to see if you really exist."

A couple weeks later I finally meet his father at another Legion dance. I've seen him before but have never been introduced. He happens to look over, and after spotting Zack standing next to me, instantly comes storming over.

"Uh, Dad? This is…" Zack hesitates for just a second, and then adds more firmly, "my girlfriend, Kathy."

I like hearing Zack say my name. His father ignores him, but looks at me up and down and then raises his eyebrows.

"Well hello there good looking!"

I can feel Zack cringing next to me. I want to tell him it's okay. I'm not afraid of his father. Not one bit. I know how to handle an asshole like him.

"So I finally get to meet the big man Zack has told me so much about," I say with my warmest smile, reaching out to shake the asshole's hand.

"Well if my son had told me what a great looker he'd landed I would've made sure we met sooner! You better make sure you save one of those dances for me tonight, 'kay little lady?"

Little lady? At five foot seven and a-half, I'm almost as tall as he is. Asshole. Zack barely says two words to me for the rest of the night. I try to hold his hand when I know his father is looking, but he pulls away.

"I'm not feeling so well," I finally say. "I'm going to get out of here, okay?"

For the next few weeks I won't take any of his calls. The shit with his father has me rethinking things. Zack has some stuff to work out, and I like him too much to let him keep being my temp boyfriend. I finally force myself to phone him.

"This isn't working so great, is it?"

He just breathes into the phone. I wonder if his forehead is creased. I try again.

"I mean, I like you and everything, but..."

"Are you breaking up with me?" he asks. He sounds shocked. "I mean, really? Did my dad say anything to you? If he did you can tell me, honestly. Really, did he do something?"

I wish I could be nicer but I have to get off the phone.

"No, your dad didn't do or say anything, Zack. Sorry, but I gotta go. Don't call me anymore, okay?"

I can hear him asking if it's because of another guy as I hang up the phone. I ignore it when the phone rings again a few minutes later.

I decide I have to go back to school. Anything would be better than cleaning up old people's shit and dating confused guys for the rest of my life. It's been more than two years since I've been inside of a school, but I know if I don't do something differently, I'm going to end up right back in the Point. I've been circling the high school near our place in LaSalle for days, my birth certificate and transcript tucked into my purse, trying to work myself up into going inside. Then I'll think about the perfect columns of F's on my transcript and angry teacher comments. What will they do? Stick me back in grade seven?

Standing outside the building, LaSalle High doesn't look anything like Westmount High. I can tell just from the outside that there aren't polished wood floors or quiet hallways. The Canadian flag out front has a bad rip on the bottom right with frayed silk threads flapping. I can see myself walking up the stairs but it's impossible to imagine past the part where the guidance counselor takes a look at my transcript.

"Oh, I see that you failed a course... and another... and another..." and then they'll realize that I've failed every single year between grade seven and grade nine.

Nobody knows I've been thinking about registering in September. I'm not sure Mom will be happy about it, either, since I've been paying room and board every week since I dropped out. Every time

I walk by the school, I remind myself that I don't have to sign up if I don't want to. If I decide to back down, that's all right. No pressure. It makes it easier to keep walking towards the school if I'm allowed to chicken out.

Standing outside the building, I watch as some students walk up and enter through the huge front doors. None of them know me. They don't know I'm from the Point. They don't know I failed every year since grade seven. They don't know that I have no clue where the fuck Peru is. They don't know anything about me. And I have a feeling they don't give a shit.

Fuck it. I step forward and move towards the large doors.

The school allows me to enroll in one of its trade programs, which means I don't have to redo grades seven, eight, and nine. Instead, I'm in a two-year cosmetology course. When I graduate next year I'm going to be a hairdresser. Yeah, it still seems funny even to me, but it was hairdressing, nursing, or auto mechanics. I already know I'm not smart enough for nursing, even if they had allowed me into the program, which they wouldn't have. And I'd rather play with hair than cars. Hairdressing turns out to be way more interesting than I ever expected. The first day I think I've wandered into the nursing class by mistake.

"This year we will be learning about the circulatory and respiratory systems and how some of the products and chemicals you'll eventually be working with can impact either or both."

No geography, history, or math. Only English and French classes, every afternoon, right after the hairdressing classes. One of the things I really love about the hairdressing course is that we're all starting off on a level playing field. There are no ace hairdressers already in the class. We're all new to the material. I almost die when I see my first report card. Not one F. In fact, I got straight As in every single hairdressing class. I almost failed French, with only a 51. But "almost" still means a pass. I passed every single fucking course. I can't wait to show Mom.

"Look at this," I say, trying to keep the pride out of my voice.

I pretend not to watch as Mom picks up the report card and studies it for a few seconds.

"God, for a second there my heart almost stopped. Then I realized all those A's are in hairdressing."

That report card gets me a part-time job in a local hairdressing salon. I realize the first day that I'm never going to cut it as a hairdresser. I hate touching other people's hair.

"You can bring Mrs. Carvey over to the sinks now, please," says the owner.

As the shampoo girl, I get to wash all the icky old ladies' hair when they come in for a tip and a fucking tail of their matted nests that get washed once a week at the shop. I always wonder what in hell might fall out as I use the jet blast cycle to give the scary parts of their hair a good soaking. I quickly learn though that a decent massage to their scalp almost always nets me a decent tip.

"Thank you!" they usually say after I wrap the towel around their fully relaxed scalp like a turban.

"When do I get to do real stuff?" I finally ask the owner.

"Real stuff?" she stares at me blankly.

"You know, like a hair cut or a perm or full set of rollers?"

I'm so bored with washing hair, I would have asked if I could answer the phone and sweep the floor, but I'm already doing that in between the shampoos.

"Oh," she says with a frown. "Well you aren't actually licensed yet and this shop only uses…"

I ignore the rest, just nodding my head. At least now I know.

Just before class starts Carrie leans over and whispers to me about this guy who she thinks would be perfect for me.

"Seriously, he is so your type. Tall, big. He's in the reserves, and goes to Concordia."

Okay, so Concordia isn't exactly McGill, but I think it's interesting that Carrie thinks she knows my type. I want to ask her a million questions but figure I'll find out most of it myself, first hand, if I agree to the double date she's suggesting.

"We'll let them take us to Adams on LaSalle Boulevard," says Carrie. "It's on the waterfront."

Adams is a restaurant that's apparently famous for it's fried liver and onions. Who the fuck has a thing for liver? And so much so that they find a favourite or best restaurant to pig-out on it?

"Okay, sure," I say to Carrie. "But I'm not eating any damn liver, right?"

The end of the week suddenly shows up and now I have to decide what a person wears to a restaurant on a first date, with a guy who apparently loves liver.

"That's perfect!" says my sister Julia.

Of course, she's already said that to everything I've shown her so I don't trust her "perfect" 100 per cent. I have to go, though, so I choose the black jeans and white dress shirt. I bought them a couple of months ago at Miracle Mart with some of my hairdressing tips and it's the fanciest outfit I've ever owned. I finish putting on my mascara and fixing my hair just as Carrie shows up. Ten minutes later we're getting out of her car. She spots her date standing outside the restaurant, a guy she's been seeing for a couple of months now, and waves. The tall guy with the crew cut standing next to him must be my date. I force myself to concentrate on walking as normally as possible. I worry my heels are going to make me do one of those embarrassing ankle bends that make me toss out my arms and give off a shriek that Mom says could raise the fucking dead.

"Hey!" says Carrie to her guy, leaning in for a kiss. I politely look away.

"Hi," says the tall blonde guy standing in front of me. "I'm Jack."

Two hours later, after choking down some liver while listening to Carrie talk non-stop about hairdressing class, I realize I'm in serious trouble. With Zack I felt strong. With this new guy I feel weak. He's talking about the last time he went camping in the middle of the winter.

"It was so cold I didn't even take my boots off when I'd crawl into my sleeping bag each night."

I ask him why he went camping in the middle of the winter. Why he didn't wait until the summer, like normal people. He throws his head back and laughs. I notice how white his teeth are. His laugh makes me grin and my stomach hurts.

"The whole point of camping in sub-zero weather," he explains, "is to challenge yourself. Anyone can camp in the summer, of course."

Of course. Sure. I do it all the time.

"Have you ever tried it?" he asks, but I know he's joking because of the smile in his eyes.

I think about what to say and then worry I've taken too long to reply. Finally, I plunge in.

"Actually, I've never gone camping during the summer or the winter. Unless you count summer camp."

"Summer camp? That's kid stuff," he says. "You should come with me sometime. I'll show you what real camping is about."

I ask him what he's taking at Concordia and he says something about political science. I didn't know politics was a science.

"What would you do with something like that afterwards?" I ask. "You know, what kind of a job?"

He laughs and says political science is just for his undergraduate degree.

"Then afterwards, who knows, right?"

I can't believe how quickly the night has gone by. Before I know it, it's time to leave and Jack insists on driving me home. As we pull up in front of my place I hope none of my sisters is peeking out the window. I panic when I realize Jack is getting out of the car.

"What are you doing?" I ask.

"Walking you to the door," he says.

When we reach the top of the stairs, he touches my arm. When I look at his hand he pulls it away.

"I like the way you seem to really think before you speak."

I decide not to tell him it's because I'm trying to remember not to say fuck or shit, and that trying to come up with replacement words takes time. It's like translating a foreign language in your head before speaking.

"I'll call you tomorrow," he says and I stop myself from rushing in to say he can't since he doesn't have my phone number yet.

"Sure," I say, hoping he didn't hear the quiver in my voice. I'm not sure if I'm relieved or disappointed that he doesn't lean in for a kiss.

"Talk to you later," he says and then goes down the stairs in what seems like one huge step.

I rush inside and race to watch him from the living room window, hoping no one suddenly turns a light on inside. He's almost at his car when he suddenly pulls off his hat off and tosses it into the air. After he catches it and sticks it back on his head, I realize I've fallen for a 6'2" Mary Tyler Moore. I could do worse.

"I need to see you," he says into the phone less than 24 hours later.

"How did you get my number?" I ask. I remind myself to breathe. I need my heart to slow down.

He explains that he got it from Carrie's boyfriend. For the next two weeks, we see each other every single night. I've never talked so much in my life.

"What are you thinking?" he asks me.

He asks it constantly, and it's getting harder to think of deep and profound things to say.

"These are for you," he says one night after he gets home from the armory.

"Why?" I ask, looking at a pair of soft brown suede boots.

"They're Mukluks," he explains. "For snowshoeing. I want to take you snowshoeing and I figure it's unlikely you already have a pair. I guessed a size seven. Am I right?"

He's wrong but I'd rather get gimpy screwed up toes than admit my feet are at least a good size larger.

"I've never been snowshoeing," I say and for once, he misunderstands the look on my face.

"They're good for wearing anytime in the winter," he says quickly. "Not just for snowshoeing."

I know that of course. Half the girls in my hairdressing class already have a pair and I'd bet my life not one of them goes snowshoeing.

"Thanks," I say, then move in for a hug. How can I tell him he's just bought me my first pair of new winter boots?

"Does this mean you'll buy me a parachute when you finally take me parachuting?" I laugh.

Jack thinks his muscular build makes him look tough and invincible. He doesn't know the skinniest punk in the Point could take him down in an instant with just one well aimed kick to his balls. His walk is a practiced one, and gives away the fact that he grew up without a father and has watched too many B-movies. With his military buzz cut and tight T-shirts, I'm embarrassed sometimes to be seen in public with him and feel ashamed for feeling that way. But his practiced walk just draws so much attention, and not for the reasons he thinks. When the metro passes through the Point he doesn't know it's my warning look that's keeping everyone off his case. I let him think it's his biceps and Dirty Harry glare glued to his face as some of the Irish gang quickly checks me out. He's safe with me as long as he keeps his mouth shut. When a young guy gets on with his ghetto blaster blaring and sits on the seat opposite us, I take a deep breath. Jack lives for moments like this. I don't know how he hasn't had the living shit kicked out of him yet. He looks at the guy, frowns, then leans over.

"Hey, Bud? Buddy?"

The young guy looks up in surprise, still not sure if Jack is talking to him.

"Wanna turn that down a notch or two?" says Jack with what he is certain is an intimidating look. A commanding voice.

If anyone can fuck up the dance of the male peacock, it's Jack. The young guy smiles and for a second I'm stunned, thinking he's actually going to cooperate. Then he cranks it to full volume. Jack instantly leans forward and turns the volume almost off.

"That's better," he says with a tight smile.

My stomach hurts. I'm ready to move when the guy suddenly makes a snorting sound and turns the volume back up. But only by a notch. Then he grunts and looks away. Jack grins at me and then leans back against his seat and closes his eyes. Now he's showing off. I like his confidence and lack of fear. The fact that it comes from his ignorance makes me nervous though. But there's so much he seems to take for granted. He assumes people have as many choices as he does. And that going to university, reading lots of books, or not being afraid is something one just has to decide to do. Or not do.

"Not everyone can own as many books as you do," I say one night as we lie tangled together on his small single bed.

"Anyone can borrow them from the library though," he says.

"Going to university isn't something everyone can do," I say another night.

"Bullshit!" says Jack and I sit up in surprise. It's the first time I've heard him swear.

When he instantly apologizes for using what he calls a "profanity," I smile in the darkness and lie back down.

He's always surprising me with gifts. Sometimes a book, one time a thin gold pen, and sometimes roses delivered right to my house. I try not to show off too much in front of my sisters. But how can I not strut down the hallway to the kitchen after some delivery guy hands me a box with twelve fucking long-stemmed red roses inside?

"You guys are doing it, aren't you?" says Julia.

Two weeks later, I go to see a gynecologist for the first time. I want to be smart about stuff and not get pregnant, but I'm embarrassed about it since seeing that kind of doctor seems to scream, "I'm probably going to start fucking soon and I don't want to get pregnant." What kind of a doctor specializes in looking at sick pussies all day, anyway? I hate to go but it's the only way I can get a prescription for the Pill. First he needs to examine me. Later I'd wonder why in hell nobody had warned me about what goes on in there.

The nurse tells me to strip from the waist down and then cover myself with a tiny sheet. The skinny couch is covered with a long strip of paper so thin, it rips as soon as I rest my ass on the edge to pull off my jeans. I take a quick look around the room and feel nervous about some of the stuff I see. Afraid the doctor will come in before I'm ready, I quickly lie down on the couch and cover myself with the short sheet. Knees or belly button? I decide on belly button and hoist the sheet up just as he enters the room. He doesn't say a word, just stares at a chart then sticks it on the edge of a counter. After plopping himself down on a small round stool with rollers, he uses his knees to pull himself over to the end of the couch. Without any warning, he's suddenly lifting my left foot and guiding my heel to rest it on a weird metal bracket, then does the same with my other foot. Now I'm spread eagle, ready for him to take the plunge. Am I being molested? Is this like what they call a fucking date rape or what? I'm too embarrassed to ask if what he's doing is normal.

"Are you currently sexually active?" says the doctor, now gently pushing down on my lower stomach.

Currently sexually active? Like right now?

"Uh?" is all I can manage to get out. I'm too busy keeping an eye on what this prick is going to do next.

"Do you have sexual relations with your partner?"

Is he asking me if I fuck my relations?

"What?"

"Do you and your boyfriend…have sex? Make love?"

Good thing the icky creep finally spelled it out for me.

"Uh, not really," I say. I'm not sure if he means naked with a penis in my vagina kind of sex. Or are we talking about hands and lips and faces? I look at the doctor and debate whether to run out of the room. He's suddenly popped a headband on his forehead with a miner's light on the front.

"What's that?" I ask, starting to sit up. I'm proud for not saying, What the FUCK is that?

"It's just a light to help me see better," he says with a smile, then sits back down on the small stool at the end of the couch.

Just when I start thinking maybe the universe is unfolding as it should, doesn't he suddenly shove what feels like a shoehorn up my damn vagina. Fuck, it hurts.

"What's that?" I demand. Please God, don't let me start crying. I decide to just leave my body.

"Sorry, I know it's a little cold," says the doctor, and then mutters weird shit about spatulas.

With that shoe horn now slowly opening my vagina, any

second now I expect the bastard to mount me. In a panic, I turn my head to the side and don't I see a whole tray of those shoehorns. They're all different sizes. After suddenly pulling out the shoehorn, my rapist jams the world's longest Q-tip into my vagina. I contemplate why one of the shoehorns looks big enough to drive a Mack truck in and another is so small, it could only be for a child. I decide I don't want to know.

"Okay, get dressed and I'll speak to you in my office," says the doctor.

He turns off the miner's light and pulls it off his forehead. After he leaves and I get dressed, I spot the light sitting on the counter. Hmm. I bet me and Jack could have a lot of fun with that.

"Here's a twelve-month prescription," says the doctor as soon as I sit across from his desk.

I can't bring myself to look him in the eye.

"Everything looks normal. Just make sure you don't smoke, even though you're young. Smoking increases your chances of blood clots when on the Pill."

Shouldn't he sound friendlier with the girl whose vagina he just explored? Maybe offer to buy me a drink? Or at least a cup of coffee?

"Thanks," I say and then reach for the prescription.

Once Jack knows I have the Pill, like a dog in heat, he can't wait to get started. I pretend to have doubts. I need to be talked into it.

"You know I love you, right?"

Yes, I do believe he loves me. He likes to sniff out every nook and cranny, licking while he explores everywhere. I force myself to stay focused. He thinks he owns me.

"I love you, too," I whisper.

"And we're going to get married one day," he says, "just as soon as we're both finished university."

He thinks I'm going to university?

"Of course!" he says.

The shock in his voice pleases me. I say I don't think I can get in anywhere with only my hairdressing certificate once I graduate.

That I haven't taken any academic stuff. Like math, or geography.

"You don't need any of that to apply to Dawson College," says Jack.

I'm almost totally naked now.

"What would I take at Dawson?" I ask. His fingers are starting to distract me again.

"Anything you want to," he says. It's time to stop talking.

Later, I can't help myself. I bring it up again.

"Were you serious about Dawson?"

He smiles at me. "What do you mean was I serious? Of course I'm serious. You're one of the smartest people I've ever met. Of course you have to go to school."

One of the smartest people he's ever met? I wonder how many people he knows? I've never loved someone so much in my life. Forget his ridiculously short hair. If his mother wasn't about to arrive home any minute, I would have proved my undying love right then and there on the spot.

"I think I'm going to fail French class," I say to Jack one day.

"Why didn't you tell me before that you're worried about it?" he asks.

From then on, every day after school, Jack helps me with my French homework. I feel stupid at first, allowing him to hear my terrible accent. But he won't let me stop.

"You need the credit to get into Dawson," he says, "and to graduate from high school. Now read that out loud to me again."

When my mark in French class goes up a lot on my next report card, Jack stops by Dawson on his way home from Concordia and picks up application forms.

"You should start looking through all of this," he says. "Think about what you might want to take."

What I might want to take? I flip through the pile of brochures then stop when I see one labeled 'The Arts and Culture.' Inside it explains that the program offers students, "...the flexibility to explore the creative arts without focusing on any one discipline, although they may choose to concentrate on only a few disciplines."

Doesn't that mean you get to just sit around and play at being a student, moving from one course to another, dropping the boring ones until you decide to focus on only the good shit? That can't be right. I read a bit more.

"This profile is a good choice for students wanting to achieve a solid background in the arts without specializing at this point in their education. Students graduating from this profile will be accepted into most university programs except science."

No way. Who the hell goes into science on purpose anyway? I turn to the next page.

"The wide perspective of this profile prepares students for university studies in art history, communications, creative writing, cultural studies, film studies, education, history, international development, journalism, literature, liberal arts, philosophy, religious studies and some professional faculties."

Well, fuck me. I don't know what the hell half that shit means but even I might be able to handle learning some art history, how to talk and write better, followed by watching a couple movies. How come no one ever told me that school actually gets easier after high school? I'd be happier than a pig in shit taking any of that stuff. Maybe I really will go to university one day. If college is going to be that easy, what the hell do they do at university? Eat peanuts and watch mimes?

I can hardly fucking wait.

The Dobson sisters.

Véhicule Press

www.vehiculepress.com